Priorities in Edu

Proceedings of a Conference held at the School of Education, University of Durham, December, 1991.

Conference Speakers:

Rt. Rev. David Jenkins
Former Bishop of Durham.

Mr. Robert Graham
Counsellor and counsellor supervisor; previously Lecturer in Education, University of Durham.

Professor David Smail
Clinical Psychologist, Nottingham Psychological Service.

Mrs. Isca Salzberger-Wittenberg
Consultant Psychotherapist, former Organising Tutor for 'Aspects of Counselling for Teachers' Courses, Tavistock Clinic.

Conference Organisers and Proceedings Editors:

Dr. Geof Alred and Dr. Mike Fleming
School of Education, University of Durham.

Cataloguing Data

Alred, Geof and Fleming, Mike

Priorities in Education (pbk)

Published by Fieldhouse Press/University of Durham, School of Education

Chapter 1 © Geof Alred and Mike Fleming, 1996
Chapter 2 © David Jenkins, 1996
Chapter 3 © Robert Graham, 1996
Chapter 4 © David Smail, 1996
Chapter 5 © Isca Salzberger-Wittenberg, 1996

ISBN 0 903380 09 9

Cover detail: *The Perspective View* (Durham Cathedral and City), anonymous artist, published in the *Complete English Traveller* (pre 1771).
Courtesy of Michael Richardson, Gilesgate Archives, Durham.

Printed by Prontaprint Ltd., Durham.

Contents

Chapter 1	Priorities in Education *Geof Alred and Mike Fleming*	1
Chapter 2	Education for Earning a Living and Education for Living a Life *David Jenkins*	17
Chapter 3	Taking Each Other Seriously *Robert Graham*	39
Chapter 4	The Experience of School - Empowerment or Oppression? *David Smail*	65
Chapter 5	The Emotional Climate of the Classroom *Isca Salzberger-Wittenberg*	81

Priorities in Education

Acknowledgements.

We would like to thank the following for their help in organising the conference and preparing this publication: Betty Fairley, Marianne Fleming, Eddie Gerard, Gerald Grace, Margaret Graham, Judith Manghan, Susan Metcalf, Cynthia Pattison, Michael Richardson, Richard Smith, Tom Taylor and Christine Wright.

Presentation:

Chapters 2 to 5 are reproduced in their original form as conference presentations. They include references to contemporary events. Use of pronouns is not intended to imply any gender bias.

Geof Alred and Mike Fleming
April, 1996

Priorities in Education

Chapter 1

Priorities in Education

Geof Alred and Mike Fleming

Introduction

This publication arises from a conference on the theme *Priorities in Education* held at the School of Education, University of Durham in December 1991. Our intention in organising the conference was to focus attention on questions of fundamental values at a time when the educational world was adjusting to the major reforms and changes introduced during the 1980s. In our view that decade, in which all areas of professional practice were comprehensively challenged by new legislation, witnessed not only a neglect of important priorities in education but also a failure to debate and discuss what those priorities might be. The world of education seemed to be in danger of attaching too much importance to notions of performance and productivity whilst giving insufficient attention to questions of value and purpose. We believe that a preoccupation with accountability and effectiveness, always important criteria, is not in itself a worthy end and derives significance only when pursued in the context of some sense of what the whole enterprise of education is for. It was this conviction that became the seed from which the conference grew. We were seeking something more than a bald statement of aims or the simple articulation of what is more fashionably known as a 'mission statement'. We wanted to encourage discussion which would explore the tensions and consequences of taking fundamental priorities seriously and which would include some scrutiny of the underlying values implicit in prevailing policies.

Thus a starting point for the conference lay in the perception of a failure to address issues of value in a manner commensurate with the scale of reform. However, we not only *perceived* a failure, we also *felt* it personally in our working lives. As teacher educators attempting to mediate between novice teachers and the wider educational world, we felt the need to reaffirm fundamental priorities and to be reminded of the wisdom, and indeed professional obligation, of remaining open to fundamental questions. We felt that the foundation of our professional practice was in danger of being shaken by the sheer pace of activity and change. Extensive interest in the conference suggested we were not being idiosyncratic.

Change in any context is likely to bring conflicting feelings; on the one hand, change represents stimulus, intellectual challenge and excitement and, on the other, it engenders bewilderment, feelings of anxiety and a sense of loss. To experience the effects of externally imposed change without the fulfilment to be derived from involvement in its inception and deliberation about its purpose is a disturbing situation to face, and one likely to lead to stress. This is precisely what many teachers have experienced in the last fifteen years. The change in teachers' contracts and working conditions, increasing centralisation of the curriculum, changes in the finances and management of schools, modifications of external examination systems and the introduction of new systems of inspection are among the changes to which teachers were subject without any real involvement in questions of purpose or control over what was happening. The ideological origins of recent reforms are there to be seen; the introduction of external systems of assessment and league tables, for example, was clearly driven by the application of market principles to education. It was not however our intention to use the conference to take a political stance on specific issues; the debilitating effect on morale seemed as much to do with the degree to which teachers lacked a sense of ownership of the initiatives they were required to adopt and implement as it was to do with particular changes. With the benefit of hindsight, and particularly in the light of the Dearing reforms[1], it is widely recognised that many of the changes were inappropriate and ill-judged. We believe this was partly because new legislation was not accompanied by a debate about fundamental priorities involving all interested parties. Clearly some changes have been productive but at the time their implementation also contributed to unnecessary stress and alienation.

Four years later the conference papers, now the chapters of this booklet, seem to us still challenging, relevant and worthy of reaching a wider audience. The pace of change has slowed and a period of stability in education has been promised. There should now be more opportunity and space for reflection and for consideration of questions of value which, although fundamental, can easily be seen as peripheral compared with the imperative to cope with the practical implementation of new policies. The demand that conferences, in-service courses and publications should provide ideas to support the application of policies rather than address more fundamental, philosophical and moral questions has been an unfortunate feature of education in recent years, albeit an understandable one, given the pressure to which teachers have been subjected.

The Conference Speakers

When planning the conference we were aware of the risks of basing it on a theme which at the time could easily have appeared remote and irrelevant to current needs. However, the attendance of over a hundred delegates on a cold Saturday in December indicated that our concerns were shared by many others. We wanted the conference to be an exploration of statements of beliefs about what the true purpose of education should be and what values should underlie its practice, and not reports of empirical research or descriptions of policy initiatives. We were also aware that our intention could easily be misinterpreted as a simple rejection of traditionalism and a harking back to a vacuous and rather woolly form of progressivism, lacking substance and rigour. We were pleased therefore that some of the speakers pointed up the unhelpfulness of false and simplistic polarisations.

It was for these reasons that we chose speakers who would offer perspectives both close to and more distant from the teaching profession. At the time of the conference none of the speakers was engaged in teaching in schools or teacher education and we felt that their contributions would transcend current preoccupations and jargon to give a new perspective and a fresh way of thinking and talking about education. We wanted to avoid what one speaker described as the 'bandying of slogans' (p. 22).

The speakers form an interesting and contrasting quartet: David Jenkins, then Bishop of Durham; Robert Graham, counsellor, and former teacher and teacher educator; David Smail, clinical psychologist; and Isca Salzberger-Wittenberg, psychotherapist. We recognised in David Jenkins someone with a natural ability to connect the conviction of his deep Christian faith with all aspects of living and someone with an unfailing courage to speak out against prevailing assumptions. His book *Free to Believe*[2] which deals in part with the distortion of truth and the betrayal and neglect of fundamental questions had just been published. Robert Graham, as well as being an experienced teacher, has considerable experience as a counsellor and counsellor supervisor. As a former colleague, we knew that his work and writing has always been characterised by an uncompromising honesty and by powerful beliefs. David Smail was known to us through his writings, especially *Illusion and Reality: The Meaning of Anxiety*[3], which generations of teachers have found valuable and empowering. He has written with clarity and insight about the experience of peoples' lives in contemporary Britain from the perspective of a clinical psychologist, often challenging deeply-held assumptions of his profession. Similarly, we first knew Isca Salzberger-Wittenberg through her book *The Emotional Experience of Teaching and Learning*[4] which has helped teachers and trainee teachers to acknowledge and respond to the emotional aspects of teaching and learning and to work productively in the emotional climate of the classroom.

Priorities in Education

It was our belief that these four speakers would each have a distinctive voice and perspective but that their contributions would complement each other and provide a truly enriching experience for the participants in the conference. We were confident they would avoid the fate of much current educational discourse which tends to be technicist and narrow. And indeed, there is little which directly addresses issues such as attainment targets or cost effectiveness, for instance. Nor is there any repetition of familiar clichés. In short, the contributions may be described as four versions of what the phrase 'back to basics', much used and misused in the political rhetoric of recent years, can and should actually mean.

David Jenkins contrasts a narrow utilitarian view of education with a rich and profound vision of what education for living a life might entail. He reminds us that the enterprise of education takes place in a wider social and political context and is necessarily and unavoidably underpinned by values. His reference to political affairs current when the conference took place demonstrates the links he makes between what goes on in formal education and what is happening in society, nationally and internationally. The two cannot be separated. Likewise, education for earning a living, a seemingly functional matter, and education for living a life, an elevating and enriching experience, are seen to be inextricably linked when priorities in education are rooted in profound human values. The chapter is both visionary and eminently practical. David Jenkins places relationships at the heart of education and considers the development of relationships a fundamental priority. This becomes an integral part of a fresh perspective on how, and on what principles, the school curriculum can be constituted.

Robert Graham sees the educational landscape strewn with unhelpful tensions and oppositions, where different approaches, views and ideologies are in conflict and, together with imposed change, threaten to alienate and disable the very people - learners and teachers - who make the education system a living part of society. For him, an indispensable way to identify and promote priorities in education is to examine what it means to take another person truly seriously. Although in common parlance this phrase is often used lightly, it encapsulates an exciting and challenging view of education. Drawing on young people's experiences whilst pupils or students, Robert Graham illustrates how formal education in so far as it fails it to engage people's real selves must to a degree fail to take them sufficiently seriously. What really matters in a person's life often lies neglected and hidden behind the appearances of being educated and the activities which apparently are the proper business of school. He too places relationships at the heart of education. 'Serious' relationships foster trust and, crucially, a sense of belonging. An education that takes people seriously helps them develop positive attitudes and genuine feelings of responsibility towards subjects and skills, and towards their own capabilities. And such an education enables pupils and students to engage wholeheartedly with what interests them and what really matters to them. The fundamental priority is to 'take each other seriously'.

David Smail approaches priorities in education from the perspective of a clinical psychologist working in the National Health Service, where the people who come for help often live lives with little hope or opportunity. He observes how seldom people who experience difficulties in adult life talk about their education and, of those who do, how seldom is school remembered as exciting or illuminating. He develops the theme that school is an irrelevance for many people given the social and economic circumstances of their lives. Education is irrelevant when it fails to engage with people's true concerns and when it fails to give a sense of connection with others and of belonging to a community. The teacher mediates between the child and possible worlds he or she might enter, be they those embodied in traditional school subjects or in other aspects of a culture's traditions and endeavours. From this perspective, David Smail identifies two central priorities in education: to help children find ways of addressing their own legitimate needs and desires through engagement with others and involvement in the material world, and to pursue the moral aim of sharing knowledge that leads to benefits for all. His chapter can be described as an expression of the moral case for comprehensive education.

Isca Salzberger-Wittenberg complements and reinforces the vision of the other speakers with a focus on the emotional dimension of everyday life in schools, and the priority of creating an emotional climate that promotes learning. Her starting point is that the emotions are often neglected in teaching. As teachers enter into relationships with pupils, they are constantly tested not only for their knowledge and skills, but also for their human qualities. Feelings of inadequacy, resignation and fear of losing control, as well as a wide range of positive feelings, are part of the emotional currency with which learners and teachers interrelate. The feelings can be powerful, and they can also be distressing, and one reaction is for teachers to look for ready made solutions. There is an impulse to get rid of the problem as painlessly as possible, to look for technical solutions, to find a quick 'cure'. Isca Salzberger-Wittenberg argues, however, that if the emotional climate of the classroom is to enhance rather than distort learning then teachers need the ability and resilience to acknowledge and contain the emotional impact of dealing with learners' feelings. Her priorities, couched in terms of teacher education, concern learning to truly listen and observe, and learning to tolerate doubt and uncertainty.

The four chapters provide distinct ideas and perspectives and also address, from differing perspectives, common themes. One theme is a concern to eschew false polarisations and to reject the mistaken view that attention to fundamentals can be set aside when dealing with the practicalities and exigencies of school and classroom life. David Jenkins' concern with rigour - 'we don't want romantics; we want facts and organisations' (p. 25) - is echoed by Robert Graham's rejection of 'crazed polarisations...such as staunch traditional values versus woolly progressivism' (p. 39) which in turn is reflected in David Smail's view that education must centrally be about a 'person's relation to a social and material world' (p. 72). The centrality of relationships is a second important theme. We become educated and come to know ourselves through the connections and relationships we are helped to make with others and with the world. And relationships can be hard work, especially when the emotional demands are not acknowledged but instead intrude, often painfully, to complicate the teacher/learner relationship.

The Professional Needs of Teachers

The conference brief did not encourage the speakers to draw out the practical implications of their views but what they say contains many implicit and explicit lessons. Many, if not most, of these focus on the learner and the curriculum. But there are also important lessons about the professional needs of teachers, and about the conditions in which teachers endeavour to make education a vital and enriching experience. For example, just as dialogue lies at the heart of learning and teaching, the introduction of new initiatives in education at a national or local level will only be genuinely progressive when accompanied by consultation which enables those responsible for their implementation to shape and own them. This basic tenet of effective management was obscured, if not totally ignored, in the climate created by radical imposed change. Many teachers have paid with a kind of *weltschmerz*, feeling themselves in pain in the world, and experiencing both profound pessimism and a yearning for something better.

Thus a discussion of values and priorities which indicate the expectations society at large might properly have of teachers leads also to a recognition of teachers' own legitimate needs and expectations and to the vital importance of supporting them as they carry out the task entrusted to them. This recognition can be vividly emphasised by recalling the advice airlines provide to their passengers, 'In the event of an oxygen failure, those of you travelling with children should first place an oxygen mask on your face and then - and only then -

place a mask on your child's face'. It is a striking metaphor when applied to the educational context - meeting the needs of learners cannot be done without or before meeting the needs of teachers, and the stakes are high.

What then is the oxygen teachers need? We suggest that new skills, new knowledge and training dedicated to the implementation of particular initiatives is part of what is required. But it is only a part, and on its own woefully inadequate. Far more important are the opportunity and encouragement to cultivate a reflective stance, to revisit fundamental issues, to value and learn to critically evaluate one's work and to be able continually to restore oneself and resume with renewed energy, enthusiasm and commitment. The priorities for effective teaching of truly listening, observing and containing identified by Isca Salzberger-Wittenberg and the fundamental importance of taking learners seriously, in the sense articulated by Robert Graham, are as vital in the staffroom and the wider context of the teaching profession as they are in the classroom, and when actively valued and promoted represent the oxygen teachers breathe.

The <u>opportunity</u> to reflect is central to being a teacher and vital to the success of the educational enterprise. Dr. Jenkins' chapter, for example, demonstrates the intimate connection between values, policy and practice, a variant of the truth that 'there is nothing so practical as a good theory'[5]. The <u>encouragement</u> to reflect is legitimately sought both from within the teaching profession itself, and also from without, through affirmation and support coming from society at large, and in particular from parents, pupils and politicians. Writing about the place of theory in the context of initial teacher education Richard Smith argues that student teachers have the right:

> ..... to be given sufficient opportunity to develop the understanding, the critical acumen and the habit of reflection without which professional life risks being a constant source of bewilderment and dismay, and to discover the sense of excitement which, quite apart from anything else, provides pupils with teachers who are living evidence of the worthwhileness of education.[6]

Teachers thus prepared are ready to teach in the deeply moral way described by David Smail, to reveal to the learner worlds of understanding and knowledge, and to mediate as the learner engages with the offerings of formal education. Again, attention to teachers' needs is intimately bound up with the ostensible and proper purposes of education.

Discussion of fundamental issues in education must include consideration of priorities in teacher education and in continuing professional development, and it must do so in terms consistent with the expectations and aspirations we have for children and young people. An instrumental, technical perspective is no more appropriate for teachers than it is for learners.

Conclusion

We conclude this introduction on an optimistic note. Although pressures on schools continue, there is no doubt that the teaching profession remains responsive and committed. The promised period of stability following the Dearing Reforms can provide an opportunity to look again at teachers' needs and expectations alongside their responsibilities. With sufficient imagination and resolve, we can find and create sources of oxygen to sustain a living and lively education system.

One potential source can be found in the recent introduction of mentoring in schools. This is primarily part of the arrangements for the induction of new entrants to the profession but could also be extended to benefit established teachers. Mentoring is at heart a relationship between two people, and its purpose is as much to prompt reflection and self awareness as it is concerned with skills and information. A mentor fosters learning and development, offers advice, insight and wisdom, and supports and protects. A certain irony lies in the fact that as a result of reforms in teacher training, experienced teachers are being called upon to act as mentors to newly qualified teachers when they themselves would also benefit from similar support. Nevertheless, there is an opportunity here for teachers to use these reforms to create a more caring, supportive environment in staff rooms, and to become more conscious of helping one another and of valuing collegial relationships. Indeed, mentoring embodies many of the priorities in education identified in the following chapters.

A second approach to sustaining teachers is to be found in the notion of the sabbatical term. In higher education, sabbatical terms have traditionally been used to increase research output and enhance academic standing. However, they serve also as periods of regeneration and renewal. We believe that if similar opportunities became an accepted part of a teacher's working life then schools and the teaching profession as a whole would be enriched and become more effective. At present over four hundred million pounds is spent on the professional development of teachers[7]. We would like to see a proportion of this sum invested in teachers' sabbaticals. A period of further study, secondment to industry or to other workplaces, or experience of schools in other countries would stimulate fresh perspectives, and bring renewed enthusiasm and energy into schools and classrooms.

At the time of writing, the Teacher Training Agency is reviewing arrangements for improving the professional development of teachers. We have identified two ways in which this could occur - mentoring and sabbatical terms - and we believe many more follow readily when teachers' professional needs are seen to go beyond mere functional training. It would be a bold step to include in a national system of teacher development genuine opportunities for teachers to take a personal initiative based on this recognition. Certainly, the insights, beliefs and wisdom of the following chapters lead us to believe that if this step were taken it would do more than any other educational reform to improve schools and to enhance the learning and futures of children and young people.

Finally, we would like to thank David Jenkins, Robert Graham, David Smail and Isca Salzberger-Wittenberg for their contributions to the conference. To encounter their voices again in preparing this booklet encourages our own continuing reflection on priorities in education.

Chapter 2

Education for Earning a Living and Education for Living a Life

David Jenkins

I start from a hopeful sense of shame. Let me explain what I mean by a hopeful sense of shame, and then I will explain why I have got it. Shame, I think, is a sense of falling short, a sense of some responsibility for, or some involvement in, something wrong, undesirable, humanly distasteful. So it is an unease at oneself and one's context, an awareness of personal involvement, shall we say, in some humane falling short. Now a sense of shame, to me, can be hopeful because of my understanding and my faith about the possibilities of the world and the spiritual resources available in it. If I may put this in what I might call Christian terms, a sense of wrongness is an invitation to repent, to rethink, to receive redirection and renewal, in a better, more humane and more promising direction. So you see, shame is not meant - and need not be received - as an invitation to be trapped in self-regarding guilt but rather can be an invitation to perceive and receive new and better ways forward.

It seems to me we cannot tackle our subject today, *Priorities in Education*, within the context in which we have been invited to consider it (all the changes of the 1980s) without being challenged. The subject quite definitely, and simply, and practically challenges us about our basic approach to life, our fundamental attitudes, hopes, fears, aspirations. There were indications in what the Head of Department[8] was saying by way of introduction, that to be practical nowadays, particularly at this juncture, you have simply got to consider values, aims, and commitments. In terms of my chosen title - even if education has practically and basically to be for earning a living (for if there is no 'earning a living', then nobody will live to live a life), there is still the question: 'and what happens when, and as, we are living a life?' - 'is earning a living what living a life is about?' It is clear to me that most of our political and practical discussion nowadays is so sloganised that the questions behind the questions are not faced. These are questions about 'What do you think about life?', 'Is it worth living, and what do you try to live it for?' And '*How* do you live it, and who do you live it with?'

So I start from a hopeful sense of shame. Shame is what I feel at the moment, this week, as an Englishman (or should I say, a British person), after Maastricht. I have always been very conscious of being an Englishman, although my name is Welsh. When in a foreign context, I feel more conscious of it than ever. I was once ill-advised enough, when delivering a lecture to the World Council of Churches in Addis Ababa, in the

Hall of African Unity, on the subject of 'what it is to be human', to forget that not everybody shares my liking for Gilbert and Sullivan. In discussing humanity and plurality I referred the delegates to the fact that I agreed with the gentleman who, in HMS *Pinafore*, sings, (I won't sing it):

> **He is an Englishman. He might have been a Russian,**
> **A French, or Turk or Prussian, or perhaps Ita-li-an.**
> **But in spite of all temptations,**
> **To belong to other nations,**
> **He remains an Englishman.**

That's me. And I am ashamed to belong to a country whose Government publicly holds to the view, in isolation from all other EEC nations, that we cannot afford to partake in a Social Charter, because it would interfere with our competitiveness in commercial and industrial markets. Most of the economically leading European nations can apparently manage it. We must, therefore, be shamefully inefficient, shamefully short-sighted and blinkered. Our managers and industrial relations personnel must be painfully incompetent, our trade unions shamefully outmoded and misaligned. Surely, if this is the case, it means that our society is shamefully at odds in a very deep and disturbing way. (And that is us; *all* of us; I am not blaming *them*. One of the most godly and practical doctrines, of which I have become increasingly aware in my theological and spiritual life, is the doctrine of solidarity and sin. It is *we* who go wrong, not them, and as like as not, *they* are either part of us, or terribly like us).

We are, I think, in a very distressing, pathetic and shameful situation. I do not think you should let it get you down, but I believe it underlines the fact that the issue of basic priorities is today very sharp indeed. We ought to be ashamed of ourselves. I am hopefully ashamed because the situation and the shame should indicate forcibly to a very wide range of people that we do indeed need to rethink our priorities in relation to basic beliefs, questions, ideals, about what it is to be human and in what sort of world. Is life about, and does life have to be about (first of all and, as it were, definitively) earning a living? Or is earning a living somehow - however vital, in the literal sense of that term - secondary to, subordinate to, subservient to, living a life? There is an obvious theological echo here: 'Man (which includes woman) shall not live by bread alone'. But, then people say: 'But what about the people who have no bread?' And the answer to that is: 'Indeed, what about them?' For the Third World poor are trapped by the First World economies to the extent that they lack bread, while other people have a lot of cake (to quote Marie Antoinette).

So, it is all very well saying: 'But if we don't do this, we shall not survive', for if you put the issue of survival in a wider context - what then?

There is a very practical and pressing question about the commonly assumed parameters of much of our present public debate, not least because of the global and local circumstances we are in. It is this increasing interaction between the mega level and the micro level which I think becomes more and more practically important. At the global level there is immense political and social uncertainty. There is the USSR - but not quite; there is Yugoslavia, the Middle East, Northern Ireland; and in the UK we have politics where nobody knows where they are going, least of all, the Opposition. Then there are all the environmental threats (which, of course, could be *promises,* because once you get down to conservation, stewardship and sharing, you might actually have a world to enjoy). There is the poverty gap of various sorts (and the statistics are, I think, quite clear about the widening nature of the poverty gap, practically everywhere). Over all this there is the very worrying context of what can only be described as financial instability and non-sense. There is the whole issue of the circulation of sheer money - unrelated to health and wealth - in face of the, I think clearly established, situation of Third World debt: that is the fact that payments from the Third World to the First World are now greater than the First World's investment and trade into the Third World. On any grounds, that is simply nonsense long before you get to morality, because such a system cannot in the end take off, it is spiralling downwards. So the notion that adjustments in the direction of the total freedom and deregulation of the financial Market is the only way forward, is the equivalent of the view of the leading Gaderine swine. I think this has to be said very clearly. It is non-sense, and I don't know what has happened to our intellectual level of argument that such nonsense is allowed to pass unchallenged in the name of being practical sense. Still, there it is.

So we have a highly turbulent mega-environment, which is clearly related to, and reflected in, a highly turbulent micro-environment. That is why, I think, among other things, you get tacking and veering such a lot in our present political decisions. Anybody ought to have seen, and most people told the Government, what would happen to the poll tax. It is not, again, just an issue of morality but of practicality. County Associations and many others warned of all the things that have happened. There is tacking and veering on health trusts. There is increasing talk of setting people free by issuing more and more regulations, and there is immense political volatility, most of it, I think, sloganised and irrelevant. That is the real trouble, debate is reduced to the bandying of slogans (I suppose it is to do with five minute broadcasts and *Any Questions* and so on). The arguments are not arguments; they are just statements from both sides. Nobody will listen to anybody else, and nobody will say why.

So there is this highly turbulent micro-environment. Now, in a situation of shame, unease, turbulence and uncertainty, the premium is, as a matter of practice, on values, vision and faith. For if things around you are tacking and veering, if your environment is upsetting, confusing and uncertain, you have to have some idea of responses which you will personally give, and responses which you will professionally give, and responses which your groups and organisations will give, to questions like: 'What do we go for?', 'What steadies us?', 'What rallies us?', 'What holds us together?' In short (as not a few organisational systems theory people have argued), in a highly turbulent environment, there is the highest possible premium on values.

What newness may we look for? This is very important if you think of the determinism of present arguments about freedom. Either, it appears, it sniffs of socialism (which is why you don't want this nonsense about social charters), or we must have the total Market (and that brings us back to Maastricht). It is obvious that the objections are narrowly ideological. They seem to echo what has come from the other side of the Atlantic, the claim that we are at the end of history, that we have now solved the major problems, all we have to do is make the Market work. The notion that either you must go this way *or* you must go that way is a form of narrow-minded determinism which shows that vulgar Marxism has won (i.e. whether you do what Marx did after Hegel by standing things on their head that way, or you do what the Market people do, by standing things on their head *that* way). It is quite amazing how far vulgar Marxism (not Marx), dominates our politics.

We are, it seems to me, at an absolutely fascinating, threatening, but potentially creative, time. There is the possibility of a more peaceful, more democratic, and sustainably shareable world, because the questions are so sharply posed. Hence the hopeful sense of shame: a sense of shame, but there is an *alleluia* in it. Therefore when we return to education, surely we must help one another to recover our **nerve**, our **faith** and our **rigour** (which is not *rigor mortis*, but extreme discipline in dealing with these things).

Our **nerve** must say to us: 'Look here, it is not inevitable that you either have chaos or sameness'. In the midst of things you must have the nerve to say, 'Look, this sheer chaos, this sheer randomness, this sheer uncertainty need not go on like this. This need not be the way in which we always do things; arguments do not always have to be conducted as they are being conducted at the moment'. If arguments go on endlessly, it is probably because the wrong questions are being asked. This is the same as paradigm shifts in science. If you can't answer a question, think about the question. Don't go on and on and on. Have the nerve to be convinced that neither chaos nor sameness are necessary.

Faith - which is to do with keeping faith with whatever ideals, care and vocation one has. It is perfectly true that people matter: we want to care for people, and we want to share with people. There are all sorts of reasons for explaining why that won't come off. David Hume[9] explained it at great length once upon a time, and Hayek[10] has explained it again more recently. Nonetheless there are certain things, surely, which we know, and we must keep faith with some sorts of ideals or visions however difficult. It is not impractical so to do, especially if you relate your faith to rigour.

Rigour. We don't want slogans, we don't want romantics; we want facts and organisation. That, incidentally, is of the greatest importance for professional bodies related to education. You must keep on documenting the facts, stating why you think they are facts, and go on presenting them and informing people. At the moment, it is difficult to get informed discussion going, but sooner or later (especially in what is supposed to be a democratic country), if enough people have enough nerve to keep on pointing out what is actually happening (not what is said in answer to questions in Parliament or on *Question Time*) then some difference may be made.

So we need a combination of nerve, faith and rigour. This is very necessary because education is so central to all that goes on; it is at the heart of how we shape our children and our students, and therefore what we are making of ourselves. It seems to me the biggest nonsense to claim that education is something that you can organise specially to produce certain commodities. This is a total misunderstanding of the process. Education is bound to shape our children and students, and therefore shape what we are making of ourselves. Education is not a service industry for individual consumers so that they can earn a competitive living (that is to say, a merely utilitarian component of a set of packages which are especially brought into focus by operation of market efficiency). Education is a common social shaping, serving and sharing so that we can work together for a sustainable, shareable and - as far as maybe - enjoyable future. One of the things we have to do, as we get back to basics and try to realign and share our priorities, is to oppose this fragmentation into different activities. Of course, you must define your spheres, but they remain interactive. To build up the innate confrontation contained in the blind faith that things can be subordinated and co-ordinated only by the Market is surely a counsel of despair.

So, if you get back to basics: 'who do we think we are?' Who do we think we are, and then how do we relate it to details? As a thought-experiment for the beginning of this conference I want to suggest that as we reconsider priorities in education, we take some sort of fundamental statement from which much, both about value and about practice, can be developed. (It may be arguable as a statement but it points in a direction). *Men and women are that which their relationships enable them to become.* This is not necessarily an optimistic statement of course, because a lot of relationships dis-enable people. It is an ambivalent statement, and it is meant to be so. Totally lonely men and women are both incapable of survival and incapable of happiness. The hermit after all has to have, I think, a very tough self which has been built up in relationships, and he or she usually has some very intensive idea about a relationship with God and the world. I don't think you can deal with your aloneness if you have no relationships. There is a lot of literature, from psychotherapeutics through to spirituality, which will show this. Without relationships, we could not speak. I have a sub-theme running through a lot of my thinking at the moment which I, being an academic and a classic of a certain sort, think of as the power of the

Logos. The ability to speak, (which goes with the shaping of thoughts and the passing on of information as well as misinformation - all these things are ambivalent) is very central to being human. The ability to speak has very much to do with the ability to control, and to develop. So the Logos as a free activity and the ability to speak is vital; and this wouldn't occur without relationships. Any civilisation and culture is a corporate one. Many of us believe that men and women are, in some real but dangerous sense, in the image of God, and there are some of us who have a belief in God that He in Himself (She in Herself, or It in Itself) is some sort of relationship. An economy is a set of relationships. ('Oikonomia' is simply the measure of stewardship and stewardship of handling an 'oikos', which is a household). What is more - let us not be ashamed of it - what is love about? What about celebration, enjoyment and conviviality?

It seems to me that we do well to have a vision, a picture and a *practice* of men and women in relationships. The 'oikos' and the economy, the city, its part in civilisation (that's Latin isn't it), and the polis, after all, is part of politics. If you are not concerned with relationships in civilisation and relationships in politics, you are in a mess. The Kingdom of God is all about *that* wherever it is (if it is). The community is that which enables the contributions and the fulfilment of all.

This is one of the reasons why we are in such a turbulent situation. As we now know forcibly (very forcibly, after the ideological divide and arguments of the 19th and early 20th century), to identify any heaven or Utopia or ideal community with anything here and now, or just around the corner, leads to tyranny and inefficiency. That is what happened under the Marxists, and I suspect (as I said), it is exactly what is happening under the Market (because this is supposed to be perfect, or as near as perfect a system as you can get).

We know that to identify our aims, hopes, visions and practical direction with any state of affairs which is just around the corner is terribly dangerous and quite ineffective. Similarly, this danger and ineffectiveness applies to all ideas, including any ideology or individualism. Individualism, as a basic notion and practice, threatens anarchy; it does not fit the nature of individuals. The one thing about individuals is they are not individualistic, or if they are, they deteriorate as human beings. It doesn't work. Look at one of the ironies about language. Consider the freedom of the consumer in a mass market dominated by media and finance. All these choices. Walking down the high street, you can choose any of these things, all of which are overpriced and most of which are useless. It is, again, a non-sense. Or consider the freedom of unorganised and fragmented individuals versus organised professional, commercial and financial powers. I was at a very interesting discussion last night (but it was private), with trade unions about Maastricht. They could bring up all sorts of examples as to how organisations in restraint of trade are in restraint of the Market and are not to be allowed organisation; but meanwhile it was assumed that in order to allow this or that financial deal this way of talking about 'freedom' was perfectly in order. It doesn't work. Just look at the waste and blindness of the unregulated Market and finance as they operate at present.

Identification with any one ideology is literally hopeless and destructive. The basic priority in education is to enable and to develop relationships: relationships which enable **growth, grasp, co-operation** and **openness.** Relationships have to be defined and directed however; you must not turn relationships into the latest slogan. **Growth** at a simply basic practical level. Human beings are the best resources we have - if we do not enable them to grow as best they may, we are wasting our resources - at the level of earning a living, working a market, developing imagination or whatever. I believe that this is all of a piece with the fact that if only each person could be his or her best person - whoopee! Personal growth contains the engine of practical resources, of excitement and imagination. **Grasp** is to do with developing the capacity to appreciate what is, what is going on, what it is about - so that you may better respond. If people are left in states of confusion, if they cannot organise their thinking or their responding, they are in limbo and are open to exploitation. You must develop a capacity to grasp things. That has to be related to **co-operation,** because at least two things are, surely, increasingly obvious. We must build our society and our ways of earning livings, and our ways of living a life, *together*; co-operation is a shared necessity. You simply can't know, experience, or be aware of the sort of things you need to do even simple tasks in the world today without other people. It is true that in certain circumstances, as Sartre says, 'Hell is other people' (that is me as well), but you can't do without them. So co-operation must go on with growth and grasp and of course **openness**.

Co-operation must be in relation to **openness**, for we are in such a situation of rapid change that innovation and adaptation is the requirement of everyone at whatever level they can manage. It is clear that employment, in the straightforward paid sense, is not going to be available, at any rate absolutely regularly and automatically, for large numbers of people, and people in employment will have to keep adapting to changes. So, growth, grasp and co-operation have to be related to openness.

Without this type of education for living a life, fewer and fewer persons will be educated for earning a living. After all, it is increasingly clear that unskilled and uncreative persons are not wanted for survival. This is something we have to face here in the North East. The number of people who are made redundant, or the number of people who drop out, the number of people who come to the end of school and discover no prospects, and, of course, the number of people who are left out by the spreading type of regulation with the effect of depreciating the value and status of social security or casual work all have an accumulating effect. It is clear that these persons are not wanted in the system. Surely it is vital we work at training all people for adapting to the new conditions and prepare them for a different sort of system. If you do not direct this retraining, this preparation for innovation in different ways, you find groups do it anyway in anti-social ways. Take a look at some of our criminal cultures. This is people developing enterprise. It is. I won't quote particular estates, but there are clear examples of highly organised tribal raiding. If you can't do anything else, why shouldn't you organise tribal raiding? If there is a free-for-all, we are all part of the free-for-all. This type of challenge has got to be faced and the process will require a certain development of people. The business of earning a living in this sort of world is very complicated and must be related to the ability to change. So growth, grasp, co-operation and openness.

The priorities, it seems to me, need to be focused on developing the capacities for relationship, and these relationships have to be related to a sort of dynamic interchange between survival, sustaining, and co-operation with celebration. There must be training for survival; that is to say to enable people to acquire skills and training both for earning a living and for adaptation to new contexts. This must go with helping people to live in a sustainable way - for we exist in a limited environment. If the only perceived limits are the limits of bureaucratically regulated funds, related to certain narrow tests, then that is reducing the concept of education to a degree which simply does not enable us to face the actual challenges of the real limits. This is paralleled in the difficult questions about the health service. Does anybody *actually* think that if we had the right sort of government we would have enough money to do all the things we want in the health service? The answer is quite plainly 'No'. Learning to live with limits is of the essence of living a life, let alone earning a living today. That is the issue of looking to sustainable forms of life. There are positive ways of responding to limits. There is the sustaining of living with the limits, there is the sustaining of developing the demands and opportunities of working together, and of growing in the sort of community and service that is required. These concerns do have to be related, and it is in pursuit of them that we have to keep our faith and nerve.

Survival and sustaining have to be related to 'co-operation with celebration'. One of the points about life is living it. It is very important to enjoy the living of life in the midst of all sorts of things. There are possibilities, as both saints and some very ordinary sorts of people have shown us, of getting a great deal of enjoyment under extremely difficult and miserable circumstances. One of the things I learned travelling around the world for the World Council of Churches was that only Europeans and Americans went into decline and got bored and frightened over difficult circumstances. People in the Third World were perfectly capable of supporting one another and enjoying life in conditions which I would find intolerable. I don't think that's romantic nonsense. It is sense that has got to be built back into education - this whole notion of not merely survival, not just sustaining, but of actually co-operating and celebrating.

To limit education or to define the aims, methods and

content of education, by that which produces the measurable increase of skills deemed by society at the moment to be useful, and that in a purely utilitarian way, is surely to *prevent* education. It is a mechanical theory which denies humanity and leads, I think, to the production of a stagnant, discontented and individualised society (which, as a matter of fact, can have little chance of flourishing in the competitive and demanding changes of the future). It is shutting us down to some thing too small that cannot live in the environment we are in. The future requires us to develop a capacity to compete - but to compete in adaptation, local survival and change. We need new skills, new ideas, new efforts, and new occupations, and the ability to enjoy ourselves in the midst of them. All this is very demanding. If we don't change we destroy - we risk a future disfigured by poverty, conflict, greed and violence.

Every single child and student needs to be helped to acquire necessary skills, the beginning of information in various fields - and above all how to *get* information - and the habits of discipline. You get nowhere without being organised and picking up the encouragement to persevere at a cost. I think the television works against this. Attention spans - the terrible flicking that goes on more and more in our television culture is, I think, humanly destructive. Unless you can attend to something for more than about 90 seconds at a time you will never get anywhere. (Of course this concern goes deeper and deeper than that. Contemplative attention to God requires great depth, patience, quietness; it can become exceedingly simple, and of course exceedingly creative and exciting - but that isn't the subject of this talk, is it?) The whole business of discipline, the encouragement to persevere at a cost, and people being able to discover early on in education the rewards of the costs, seems to me, to be very important - but we will no doubt hear about that from the practitioners and experts.

We need broadly agreed and widely applied common curricula. If we get back to basics about priorities to do with relationships, survival, sharing and celebration, then we can then work together at consequent details. I get this impression from outside the profession, we must overcome what seems to be almost a furious ideological interest-centred battle reduced to slogans; something like: 'child-centred care versus subject-centred education'. There seem to be foolishly slovenly models around. On the one hand, in the 1960's they invented 'child-centred classes' where the little dears do nothing but express their inadequate and untrained selves; on the other, 'we will pull ourselves together and we shall have subject-centred classes where the little blighters sit in rows and jolly well learn what they need to learn, so that they can cough it up when required at testing time'. This is the impression I get. It is absolute nonsense, isn't it? Absolute nonsense. We need renewed insights about basics related to co-operative ways of working out, trying out and modifying practice. We need to be educating persons in relationships, skills and information so that they can develop as collaborative, contributing citizens with the ability to participate in the development of the sort of world we have today. I take it, of course, that the agreed curriculum will include reading, writing and arithmetic, but not as mechanical achievements for employees, servants and manipulators of the Market. Everyone in our modern society must be able to read competently and write adequately, not so they may become employable, but so that they may become empowered. If people cannot read, or cannot write, they can neither find out nor probe nor apply. They are totally at the mercy of the manipulation of the media and commercial advertising. The equivalent of arithmetic seems to me to be some sense of calculating, of being sensible about orders of magnitude and the like. If we do not teach our pupils to develop that ability - how are they to know whether the person at the checkout of the superstore is not cheating them to the order of ten, or something like that. Simple things like this. Unless people can read, 'rite and 'rithmetise in some way or other they are totally disempowered and are unable to make judgements of comparison. If you can't make judgements of comparison, choice is a nonsense and means you are at the mercy of people who are manoeuvring your choice. So I don't think there's any doubt at all that of course reading, 'riting' and 'rithmetic are at the basis of education. It is a question of what you do it *for* and *how* you do it. (This returns us, I think, to this matter of the Logos again).

Further, I should have thought that any general curriculum needs some history and some geography in it (or that is what I would have called the subjects myself). People need to be able to *locate*. They need it more than ever when - as is the case - we live in a turbulent world, a pluralistic world where the backgrounds of some of the pupils in the school are mainly located in history and geography elsewhere. Elements of history and geography are very necessary to a rounded education, but these elements need to be designed, not in an old-fashioned backward-looking way, but - to use one of the words which is current in Christian jargon - 'ecumenically' (which, of course, simply means to do with the inhabited world). Our nation is not the centre of the world, nor is any other nation; there must be a way of doing history, and a way of doing bits from what I would call geography, which locate people in their identity and tradition within what is going on now. The *responsibility* part of this is to do with helping people to discover what has to be built, what has to be conserved, what has to be sustained and shared (for instance in relation to Europe and the Third World). So you need something which excites children about one world and our common future - of course on the basis of traditions, but not shutting us up in the past. If to be an Englishman means learning to take a nineteenth century view of what the eighteenth century was like, then it may well be destructive to be an Englishman. But, ideally, you should be (in my case) an Englishman who is open to what England means and to all sorts of other experiences and perceptions. Hence also, the necessity of finding space for languages, it seems to me. Where possible both an understanding of English (because manipulation of language is power) and another foreign language. My children (the younger pair) were brought up in Geneva at the Ecole Communale and discovered, simply by playing, that for instance there were different sorts of alphabets. Rebecca came in and drew an 0 with a line through it and that was 0 (she had been talking to a Norwegian). The experience of being with people of other cultures and languages actually means you discovered that there was a difference, and it was a good thing. Can that be brought into teaching about history, the uses of language, and the location of people in our society today from different cultures? There are opportunities, I think. Opportunities which are also essential for modern life, survival, growth, co-operation and celebration.

And, finally, there must be a place (mustn't there?) for sheer self-expression, celebration, creativity, and (if I may put it so) experiences of going beyond ourselves (if I were being professional I would call it transcendence). That is why curricula must have in them clear spaces for games, art, music and knowledge of faith. These are not subjects you tack on the end; there must be recognised spaces for them. I get increasingly bothered about the way the grasp of 'The Curriculum' extends to everything school children do now. If you come and see Auckland Castle or go to Lindisfarne, it must be part of a clearly defined historical project - that sort of thing.

If we are to get together to work on this there is an immense need, not only of a sense of direction and hope, but also of building up trust, discipline and mutual accountability. I think one of the saddest things about the present situation in many of our institutions is that there is no trust. It looks as though people who 'know all' are laying down regulations which people who don't 'know all' and have misplaced their efficiencies must keep to. This confrontational and suspicious view of life encourages the setting of parents and teachers against one another; if you don't get a certain sort of result then parents will complain. This is dreadful. This is, surely, the denial of any decent education. If children are to be educated in decent relationships, then education must be carried on by people exercising decent relationships. There is the most immense need, it seems to me, to restore trust between partners. Of course all professional bodies exploit their professions. If you have power over things that are important to people, of course you are tempted to get the benefits out of it and perhaps you use them in an exploitative way. Professionals need checking as much as anyone else - but *only as much as anyone else*. Professionals also have their pride, their calling, their skills. We need a partnership between professionals, parents, government, and funding bodies (if they are other than Governments). Such a partnership has got to be worked out in a discipline of mutual accountability. But *mutual* accountability. Not some mechanism of 'accountability' as designed by some mysterious bureaucrat with a set of regulations which he just ticks and then you're in or out, but a team, drawn from all interested parties, working together at the business of mutual accountability. And that, being a believer in *medias res*, is the right place to stop.

Chapter 3

Taking Each Other Seriously

Robert Graham

I think if I were teaching now, I would probably be trying really hard to keep my head down and my humour up, struggling flat out to minimise interferences and get on with the job, as I understood it, as best I could. I would probably find myself switching the TV and radio off whenever another item about education cropped up - a change, a new initiative, a further categorical imperative. That would probably just about involve enough jumping up and down to keep one reasonably fit, when so many crude oversimplifications and mad, spectral polarisations are stalking the land, and old bogeymen and scapegoats are rising up, and walking abroad.

I am not going to deal specifically with them in this paper, the bogeymen, the crazed polarisations, such as Staunch Traditional Values versus Woolly

Progressivism, or being a proper teacher in front of the whole class, as opposed to letting everyone do their own thing in trendy little groups, that sort of stuff and nonsense. Anyone who knows anything about education knows that to get stuck in those mythological Arctic extremes is to lose touch with virtually everything, all the vast extent of the fertile middle ground where pretty well every way of teaching and learning can have its place and weave in and amongst all the others, to everyone's advantage. I want to look instead at the idea of us taking each other seriously, since it seems to me that if we could manage that rather better, we might just about be able to put all those poor old simplifications and polarisations, and the bogeymen and scapegoats, into a long, deep sleep.

Let us start somewhere specific, quite a lot of years ago now, after a seminar for postgraduate education students near the end of their year's course. What I quote is quite unattributable, but I have left some parts out to make doubly sure, because I still feel highly solicitous towards it. I have been given a fair few confidences in my work, but not many that have moved me more, or felt more enriching.

This one came in the form of a letter pushed under my door ten minutes or so after this group's final meeting on the course.

> There are so many things that I haven't said and written. I feel that I have failed myself because I have denied myself the opportunity

to search, create, explore. I was lazy and I was frightened; frightened that if I did search there was nothing to reveal. I feel ashamed of my intellect, my consciousness - it seems so lacking. Or maybe it's there and I haven't worked hard enough to find it. How do you stop living on the surface? I'm too scared to take risks and yet I hate the anonymity of being part of the silent majority. I've failed to allow myself an existence. I feel angry, disappointed and yet alive. For the first time I'm writing with feeling. The piece of work I'm handing in is another example of my harnessed self. It reaches nowhere and uncovers nothing. It satisfies the university's regulations and nothing more. I realise it's another mask behind which I've hidden and regret it. I wanted the opportunity to explore and develop, yet I was afraid to catch it, afraid it might sting. Yet it is because the opportunity has gone, because it no longer threatens me, that I can begin to understand. So often in groups I tried to understand other people's thoughts, that it blocked my own. Seduced by other ideas I lost the pride in my own and abandoned them. I wasn't strong enough to connect with other people because my self was fragile despite the covering of many veneers.

Many years ago, I swore to myself that I was never going

to take any more exams in any shape or form whatever, and I am just in the process of breaking my promise. This June, I take GCSE German. I have joined a class at a nearby college and, young and old, we stumble along together, for the most part very happily. I allow myself to take the exam because, much as I want to get a Grade One so that everyone knows how clever I am, the truth is I don't really mind a scrap what happens. Nothing hangs by it that is going to do me any damage, practical or psychological. I do not define myself and no one defines me by how I do in it. I am not in danger.

But being on the receiving end of education can be fearfully dangerous. I'm lucky, I'm getting a chance to play with the old ghosts. They certainly make their appearances though, clanking their skeletal bones. 'She's only put *gut* on my homework this week and not *sehr gut* - what did Glenys get? And old John across the table has written more than me and there's less red pen on it.' A question to the class? 'Ask me, please! I know the answer and I will stun everybody with the splendour of my German pronunciation.' And, of course, if I don't want to be asked, all the old routines come back across the decades to my rescue - I am suddenly absorbed by the map of Germany on the wall, or rifling through my school bag with furious concentration. Chastening or entertaining to contemplate (depending on how you look at it), but this is the really fascinating conflict that sweeps back over the years, that ancient and eternal struggle at the very heart of learning, at the very heart of growing up indeed; am I learning in order to provide myself and others with indicators of my learnedness, short term ones like *sehr guts* and longer term ones like letters after my name, or am I learning in order to stake out claims in new territory and bring these into harmonious relationship with the rest of my stakes in and true connections with the world? Am I learning for show or for real?

Which takes us back to the letter pushed under my office door - a harnessed self, ashamed of its intellect and consciousness, uncertain, what is more, of their very existence, producing work to satisfy regulations and nothing more, work which reaches nowhere and uncovers nothing. Interesting words those, *reaches* and *uncovers*; they will certainly go nicely with the idea of learning *for real* rather than *for show*.

But this particular education on that afternoon all those years ago evidently didn't feel as if it had been very much for real, 'I've failed', 'the opportunity has gone'. The aching, sad words get pushed under the door, and that's that. Except that it isn't, of course: 'for the first time I'm writing with feeling', 'I feel angry, disappointed and yet alive'. And one asks oneself in the light of such words as those about the changes and the initiatives of recent times in the educational world. How far do they have at the centre of their priorities the intention of actually helping such a learner become better able to fill his or her experience of learning with a sense of felt life, instead of that travesty of dutifulness which leads to the cul-de-sac of a harnessed self, highly trained to turn out regulation satisfying artefacts? Or on the other hand, not a lot of good at doing so at all.

Priorities in Education

Here let us meet a rather dreadful young man whose way of handling the fears and humiliations he has experienced as a learner (and we have all experienced them) is rather different from that of the conformist who constructs a harnessed self to do the job. Presumably he had given the conformist way as good a try as he could earlier on and it hadn't worked out for him; perhaps he had learned to give it up even before he had got as far as starting school.

> School has never been my strong point but it's a thing you have to live with.
>
> I first attended an infant school which was all right. All the teachers were a bunch of old bags I hated them. After lunch or break they used to come in the classroom stinking fags and coffee. I think harf the time they were never Intresed in what they were doing. They always piked on me to read out when they knew fine well I couled not read. it just mack me look a fool. I can remember one teacher in the 4th year who every firday aftarnoon she whould show us her skrap book of hollydays phographs. she say I'v been hear and I'ev been ther as she turned a globe of the worled round.
>
> The posh bitch had been every where. I am shur she would have said I'v been to the moon if she thort we would have belived her.

... In the third year was good I liked the teacher so I would behive untill one day a sicolligis come to see me and interviewed me made me read ask some silly questions and sent me bake to the classroom. I spent a whole aftrnoon whith her. I did nat know what to think. I was never tould what she whonted.

That night I got no sleep by wondring what they were going to do. I was alwayes the thike one in the class. I thort they were going to sened me away.

And one day a cared was sent to the house.

Saying she was coming to see us. I had a lot of expling to do because I had nere taled my mum or dad. So she came to our house and explaind she wonted to see why I was not progresing at school.

This whent on untill the second year of this school.

That studip cow probly let me cace drag on so shwe could get more money. I'm shure I urned her a lot because every year she had a new car.

There's something rong some where isn't there.

finely I monve to the comp. which has been good and bad. up to now I hated school but you have to take the good whith the Bad

one last thing some school are bad other are good but for the bad one's they should have on the school door

> This school can
> seirsly damige
> your chileds helth

> Durham county councle

Again one wonders which, if any, of the changes and initiatives of recent times in the educational world make a priority of trying to help learners to disentangle themselves from wretched, crippling learnings such as this boy's flat knowledge that he is 'always the thike one in the class`. Or, indeed, another piece of learning I came across not so long ago in my counselling work. 'What was school like for you?' I asked this person, who evidently didn't think much of herself. Back over 20 or 30 years she reached, and came up with this, 'Oh, school! I spent all my time at school trying desperately never to make a mistake'. Some way of learning!

Back to our dreadful boy however and his reference to 'your chileds helth'. He certainly does seem to be on some journey in the direction of health when he is writing this. He sounds distinctly alive, like the student when she wrote her words and pushed them under the door.

I should perhaps say at this point, in case there is a risk of my being typecast as some sort of post-60s rather soggy liberal (indifferent to bad spelling to boot), that I do not believe taking each other seriously in education has any necessary connection whatsoever with being liberal, assuming that that might be taken to include being forever kind and forbearing, and holding a belief that everything that passes for some sort of self-expression simply must be wonderful and ought always to be given ten out of ten. There is nothing soggy about it at all, not the real thing. Nor is there anything stupid when the priorities actually in place, even though they may be hidden from view, frequently seem to require one to substitute for a person one could have taken seriously, and who might well have returned the compliment, a sort of malevolent scarecrow, distinctly threadbare, but occasionally pretty scary and well deserving of a few savage pecks.

Here now is a 5th year girl in a comprehensive school, writing a diary as part of her English course. She takes suicide as her theme; 'Monday, 10th July, God I am sick, I've no-one to talk to. Nobody understands. Baby John has done nothing but cry all day. I could kill him never mind myself.' Mother is no help to her, nor is the weather. Each day she buys a few more pills from the chemist. The rain teems down, all hope irrevocably drains away. It's a bit like reading the last pages of *Jude the Obscure* on a miserable day when one is in especially

Priorities in Education

low spirits already. By the next Sunday the end has come, and with a poignancy that Dickens himself might have relished.

> <u>Sunday 16th July 1980</u> Before I die whoever reads this diary please understand why.
>
> My dear son John.
>
> You should now be at an age to inderstand this letter. I am deeply sorry that I couldn't bring you up, John. I had you at a very young age. in fact I was 15 when I had you. I hope you will grow up to be fine big lad, someone who knows how to look after thereself not like me I was incapable. John if you go steady with a girl please treat her good and if she was to fall wrong look after her and show that you care for her. Look after yourself John and I hope you have a happy healthy life.
>
> love, Your mam never forgotten and will be always watching over you.
>
> p.s. I enclose a photograph of me.

Whatever one thinks about that, it would be difficult, going back to those two words again, to say that she wasn't in her teenage way doing some real *reaching* and *uncovering*, inwards and outwards: truly creative play with ideas and language, it seems to me, out of the felt reality of her own life as she experiences and understands it.

Given the actual deprivations she experienced and wrote about in a later autobiographical piece (a 17 year old mother who couldn't keep her, then put in a home, then adoption into a marriage where, in her words, 'I wasn't too young to understand that my dad was beating my mother up ... and they were divorced when I was seven years old'), it is not surprising that she herself gets pregnant at the age of 16, is persuaded by her own mother to have an abortion, comes to the conclusion that that was a rotten idea, gets pregnant again, has the child this time and keeps a firm grip on it. That story with all its repercussions is still being lived out in amongst all the other stories in the world: some a lot less dramatic and more user-friendly no doubt; none of them of course deserving any more or any less of being taken seriously.

Our malevolent and scary scarecrow though gets decidedly pecked in some of her pre-GCSE school reports which I certainly do not quote out of any malevolence towards report writers; many of us have probably written screeds about other people whose stories and essential preoccupations we have not really known very much about, and evolved a fair few marks we would not want to go to the scaffold for too. You've got to write a report? You write it - on the evidence available. Here are a few extracts: 'Given her dreadful attitude I feel that any teaching in this subject is utterly wasted on her'; 'a last effort in the remaining few months would at least give some chance of getting an acceptable grade'; 'she cannot concentrate for longer than a few minutes - will have to make every effort'; 'in class she is all too content to do as little as possible and has to be constantly told off for silly childish behaviour.' What is the poor housemaster to do with all this? If he's got to write a summing-up he does it - on the evidence he's got; 'If the comments on this report and the results of most of her mock exams are any guide then I am afraid that she will leave school in the summer with very little evidence of success in the past 5 years'.

What initiatives could we encourage and what changes could we make right now in our education system that would enable us to take one another, in all our immeasurable complexity, genuinely seriously? It certainly isn't easy to say which of the actual ones have had that as a central priority, assuming one takes it to include requirements such as the enriching of relationships in education, and the deepening of people's sense of belonging and of being properly placed. Some of the coarser ideas (for instance, to do with league tables, inspections, ways of picking out the best classroom performers to give them more money) do rather seem much more likely to lead, not so much to richer and subtler opportunities for us to learn to take each other seriously, as to more stringent requirements that we allow the actual connections between us to rust while we spend our most vigorous attention on oiling the appearances.

Taking each other seriously of course is a lot more to do

with having and cultivating attitudes than making and implementing initiatives, it is to do with the way we think and feel about each other. If in educating and being educated we really are concerned with doing things like *reaching* and trying to *uncover* and so on, we are not going to be too enthusiastic about initiatives that seem to require of us such a deal of making and recording judgements about people. You can walk all round people and all over them, institutions too; and you can sometimes make pretty shrewd and accurate judgements and observations, but if you only see with the eyes of the judge or the observer all you see out there are objects, things, and that way you may perfectly well miss everything about them that matters. It truly is hard if you find yourself turned into Examiner, Inspector, Presiding Judge over anything (and certainly not least establishing, say, who is to get the extra cash for being the deserving teacher) to be able to apprehend and work with the realities that always lie behind as well as amongst the appearances of things. Those school reports about the girl who wrote the suicide diary, they certainly say some objectively accurate things about her GCSE prospects. But the girl herself? They miss virtually everything that matters behind the appearances, and say nothing at all that is going to be of the slightest help in untangling the confusion and mess that her education has turned into. There is nothing there about the whole and real her.

Maybe seeing more into the truth of things behind the appearances might have made things a lot better for that 'thike' boy too, whose teachers all picked on him to read in order to make a fool of him because they knew fine well he couldn't. Which they didn't of course. He turns them into malevolent appearances, into Objects, as it seems they sometimes have done him. In so far as they and the 'sicolligis' and the parents and all the rest of us fail to hear, and make at least enough sense of his and each other's experience, so, inevitably, we end up simply unable to take each other seriously. We miss the reality behind the appearances, plunge into crazy objectifyings and end up with all variety of monsters of our own making. Rather like nineteenth century adventurers in the great dark African forests, encountering hairy beasts beating their breasts and baring their teeth, we shoot first, and find out a lot later, if at all, that gorillas are actually a rather amiable bunch with a great deal going for them.

So how about initiatives and changes that might really help us to see each other less as Objects to assess, appraise, quantify, write reports on, and all that, and enable us to do more seeing each other whole and taking each other seriously. Martin Buber[11] has a phrase that lodges in the mind. He is exploring the total difference between experiencing a person, or indeed anything out there, as an Object, and experiencing them as wholly them, something quite Other, that is, about which for that moment, however fleeting, all judgement and all objectification is entirely absent. At such a moment, he says, 'they fill the Universe', and that's about how it is. Perhaps one could say that knowing, not necessarily consciously, that you can and indeed have filled the universe for another is as good a way as any of defining that basic trust towards life which many thinkers and writers about the human condition tell us is so much the most important thing we learn, or fail to learn, in the earliest passages of our lives. We can put up with quite a lot of knocks, dismissive objectifications, and assessments that completely miss who we actually are if we have enough of that commodity. Labels stick a great deal more adhesively to those who haven't.

And now to a trainee student doing a teaching practice in a comprehensive school and having a pretty miserable time: basic trust system a little weak at times and in need of hard work and careful attention. If she gets enough support however and is taken sufficiently seriously it should just about hold. Some time after her demoralising experience she settled down to write about it.

> J and I had a student supervisor whom we saw every Friday morning. When we arrived there for the first time we were handed folders with our names on and shovelled pieces of official paper about discipline procedures, year tutor records and the like. Mrs. S. talked about the bits of paper, and then seemed to worry about what to do when they were dealt with. She always seemed to be rushing around and being terribly organised .... On the second Friday she showed us the sheet she would use to assess us, listing all the things we would be marked for, 1 to 5 for each .... One day

when she had to alter arrangements to see me she handed me an official form detailing time and place. .... I remember feeling a mixture of disbelief, anger and dread.

Mrs. S. comes in to observe and assess a lesson, and everything goes wrong. Most of us know or can imagine the nightmare scenario: the books and equipment that were so certain to be there one didn't check - and they aren't; the confidence draining away; the blank terror. The lesson gets a mighty rollicking and on the face of things probably deserved it. The student's comments on the effect of the rollicking certainly bear listening to however, especially this bit: 'It implied', she says, 'that I did not feel any sense of responsibility for my own actions and that I needed telling off like a disobedient child. It pushed me towards irresponsibility.'

Student/teacher horror stories, from both perspectives, are common enough, of course, and that fact itself is clear evidence of the problems and complexities inherent in what is inevitably such a difficult transition time - evidence too of the sensitivity and subtlety required from all parties if such times are to be lived through sufficiently well.

'It pushed me towards irresponsibility'. That seems to be a pretty good indicator of an educational priority. It might go something like this:- no initiative in education should ever lead people - teachers, pupils, any of us - into feeling 'pushed towards irresponsibility', like disobedient children. It is like saying, as one tends to at such times, 'all right then, if that's the treatment I'm going to get, stuff it, someone else can carry the can'.

Some ex-colleagues of a teacher friend of mine, teaching in a large Primary School where my friend spent some of her happiest and most creative years in a long career, found notes on their desks in their respective classrooms a year or so ago, put there by their new head. The messages were clear and terse: under no circumstances were they ever to leave their classrooms during lessons, not any. Then followed precise information on the exact times after which they must not arrive in the classroom and before which they must not leave it. How can such essentially frivolous treatment of people not have at least a substantial heave at pushing them towards irresponsibility? What can one say of initiatives and behaviours that, at least in their consequences, seem to make the treatment of people as irresponsible objects a priority?

I have a fear of being interpreted here as saying something really soggy, namely that the supreme priority in education is that we should all be lots nicer to each other. In a profound sense that is entirely true but it is obvious nonsense if it precludes us from telling the truth, as we see it, to our pupils and students, and to each other about how we are respectively doing our work; also if it precludes us from making decisions and taking action that might cause discomfort or even distress, all activities that can really cost, and which usually call for a lot of courage and hard work. The distinction I am making is not between being nasty to people or being warm and loving, it is between proceeding by enacting initiatives that appear to require people to jump to it and learn new tricks, and, on the other hand, proceeding by working with people in such a way that they have a stake in what is going on and know it, and therefore feel a real sense of belonging rather than alienation. And in addition to a feeling of belonging, since you cannot feel belonging in something without caring about it, a sense of responsibility as well. If you fire initiatives at people you can certainly make them hop about and try to do your bidding; like power crazed bullies in a Wild West movie you can empty your six guns into the dust all round their feet. Their leapings around will only raise even more dust though. Those teachers who were sent the dictatorial notes, after their preliminary hurt and anger, were able to settle things for themselves and retain their sense of belonging and their responsibility because they had enough self-respect and mutual regard to be able to take each other seriously. The student, destined for division by assessment into several times five parts, set about reversing her push into irresponsibility by getting to grips with the experience through the hard, brave and extremely interesting work of trying to tell herself the truth about it.

This is where she ended up;

> So that is the terrible monster of teaching practice. What can I say now? Just that it is such a relief to be able to get it down like this, and that, yes, it really is working. A feeling of some frustration, the crudity and weakness

of my words, and the need for more words, better language, to speak and understand better. A sense of really working and really growing that I have got from this course, a feeling that I have been getting recently, through a lot of time spent talking and writing, that words are getting back their power. I seem to have been so silent in the world for so long.

Through this piece of work I seem to have moved from an almost indulgent inwardness to a kind of outwardness and strength. I started hesitantly, not knowing where I was going but ended up going somewhere. I started with only a knowledge of my own guilt and depression and found some sort of strength and trust in myself, found what was good and hopeful in teaching practice, and the only thing that could enable me to go on with teaching.

As misery and guilt give place to re-engagement and interest in the process of becoming a teacher again, she begins to claw her way back to a sense of really belonging, and feeling responsible about it. From that firm and realistic base it begins to make sense for her, and those working with her, to start making assessments about where she is in the process and where she needs to go next.

Although it is harder to do and involves more honest

uncertainty than we often admit, it does make obvious sense to think in terms of standards, and find ways to assess people's competence where training for many activities in the world is concerned and that certainly includes teaching; but must we go on trying ever harder to apply that way of doing things right across the board? How about a policy initiative whose priorities included trying to eradicate factors which damage people's sense of belonging in their learning and push them towards irresponsibility? Such an initiative might even have the wonderful consequence of helping us all understand that the real value of a learning experience, in any area of study, not only does not have to be subjected to trial by measurement, but that such trial may stand a very good chance of hopelessly obscuring or worse still seriously violating such value as might have been gained from its study.

At which point I will follow Cardinal Newman's assertion that in some cases 'egotism is true modesty'[12], and tell the reader that I once came top in a school exam in Physics late in my 4th year of secondary school. I managed it because I was scared stiff of the teacher who had a terrific reputation for savagery, such as running electric shocks through entire classes and waving his razor strop around with apparent intent to use it. I had no belonging whatever in that experience of learning Physics, nor, of course, could I possibly have felt any responsibility towards the world of Physics. My relationship with it was as rooted in reality as History is in *1066 And All That.* Yet I must have attained many a target, and even sailed on from the odd key stage - in a pretty leaky and oarless boat, be it said. Naturally, if I had not been scared stiff as I swept my way from one suspect attainment to the next, I might have ended up with some genuine belonging in that major realm of human understanding and exploration, instead of finishing up quite stupid about it and switched off from it.

I have no spectacular musical talents either, yet far from being stupid or switched off about music my belonging in it is one of my solidest connections with life. I have, thank goodness, a minimal history of being measured in it and found either wanting or a lot smarter than I really am. My learning has mostly enabled me to get embedded in it in ways that work for me, and I hope for others with whom I have sometimes made music and often shared a passion for it. Because I have never been very much detached from reality in my connections with it, I am good enough to know my measure. I know enough about what being really good at any branch of it would entail, and I delight in encountering mastery that I could never get remotely near. That I turned out after 10 years of lessons to have no significant talent as a pianist has not mattered at all. I have my place in music all right, I belong in there with Alfred Brendel, John Lill and all the rest, and I enjoy that very much and am very grateful for it. I belong in golf too, for all my frequent duff shots, with the likes of Nick Faldo and Arnold Palmer (to name a special hero). And so did John Betjeman, of the utterly memorable birdie when 'The very turf rejoiced to see/ That quite unprecedented three.'

Thanks to that belonging I do not have to fall into myths of being a star when I am not, or of being the 'thike' one who doesn't deserve to belong - I take myself entirely seriously in those areas of my life and have the right to do so. The standard reached has scant connection with the rightness of the belonging, or with the sense of responsibility one has to a territory where one belongs. I was spared the experiences that led me to a crazy knowledge of unbelonging in the world of Physics, and plenty of other worlds too. I would far rather have been a fairly inept and yet essentially belonging member of the DIY world than the peripheral figure I am, equipped with little more than a tedious line in jocular self-deprecation. It has to be said though that it is a lot more comfortable to end up as an outsider to the DIY world than it is to end up an outsider to one of those worlds to which, for various reasons, an almost moral worth gets attached, and absence from which might make one feel an outsider indeed. I mean the worlds, for example, of language and maybe soon of Information Technology and I am thinking here of the sorts of experiences quite a few people I have worked with in counselling must have had to lead them to their extraordinary, nonsensical and crippling convictions about themselves. 'I was no good at school'; 'I'm no good with words'; 'I'm just useless at communicating'. Just like that, pitchforked into the exclusion zones. And what do we human beings get up to when we experience such drastic exclusion from belonging? All variety of activities and inactivities; but one way or another, for sure, we make havoc.

When the mass of children start school knowing fine well that they belong, and then end it, many of them, in a world 'cabin'd, cribb'd, confined'[13] and full of no-go areas and no entry signs, our priorities and our reforming initiatives would indeed seem to have sent us down some arid and stony paths.

Of course, what happens to people's sense of belonging and to their trust in themselves and others, does not just depend on their education. Simply to be alive is potentially to be exposed to fearfully damaging experiences as well as marvellously enriching ones. Teachers could not possibly simply stuff their pupils with goodies, even if, to purloin Dickens' metaphor from *Hard Times*, filling up all the little empty pitchers were the universally agreed aim of education. A lot of the pitchers have highly problematic contents and blockages in them even by the time they have lined up for the first day of school. Teaching, as we all perfectly well know, is difficult, and also much more interesting precisely because it is not a simple matter of transmitting things and then testing to see if the transmission has been successful. It is about being endlessly inventive in finding ways, necessarily often very different ones for different people, to help the making of real connections between what is being studied, and, to extend the Dickens metaphor, what is already in those pitchers - fermenting, lying dormant, or doing whatever it is doing. Things either get properly digested or they do not, and the latter state of affairs can have messy consequences.

Where then are we to look for the educational initiatives of recent times that really are of value to us in the heart of our work, the ones for example whose priority really is to help people make living connections between what they learn in school and all that they already know and have become? Where are the initiatives which show that we know perfectly well that to chop learning up into a vast quantity of targets to be attained and skills to be mastered is just fine in so far as education is about seeing to it that things get done efficiently to a lot of Objects out there, but that that really does have its limitations? And what about the policies and initiatives designed to help us all to develop the mutual support and trust, and the feelings of purpose and of value that might even make all the proliferating bureaucratic tasks seem more bearable but would probably more likely help us know more clearly which ones had better be thrown out or allowed to wither away.

And, finally, what of the policies and initiatives that will help us with the supreme priority, namely taking each other seriously, seeing to it that those 'Objects out there', by which I mean all of us, don't exclusively experience themselves exclusively as 'Objects out there', that they don't end up 'thike' or 'harnessed selves' or driven 'towards irresponsibility', that they don't go through school with their real life concerns unrecognised and unacknowledged, that they don't end up in unbelonging, in the midst of no-go areas that they either skulk past or sneer at or would prefer to smash up if they get the chance. We do not want or need to do such things when we know, and when our contact with others confirms our knowledge, that we are not simply 'Objects out there' and that in the long run the assessments and the labels do not describe or circumscribe us, that we really are pretty mysterious, and illimitable way beyond the limitations we will try and impose on each other in the world of education - and in the whole wide world too.

How about a new school rule to finish with: that no educational change or initiative (assuming of course that we really do need it) should ever be allowed out to work and play amongst us unless and until it truly understands how to take us seriously, and is penetrated through and through with respect and proper uncertainty; and knows absolutely, and is well content in the knowledge, that we are all of us infinitely beyond and other than the sum of our assessable parts.

Chapter 4

The Experience of School - Empowerment or Oppression?

David Smail

I have found a good rule in life to be that if one doesn't know what one is talking about, one should best keep one's mouth shut. This looks like being yet another of those occasions when I am going to find myself breaking that rule. For it is difficult to see what a clinical psychologist who has no professional or formal involvement with schools could have to say about priorities in education which could lay claim to any serious attention - especially from people who *are* professionally involved in teaching.

The way I have tried to approach the subject, anyway, is to think about it from an angle I *do* know something about, and that is: what the people who come to consult me professionally seem to find and to have found significant about their education, especially in relation to the issues they consult me about. Perhaps I should say just a few words about who those people are.

The great thing about a public health service is that,

even though very inadequately and too often only potentially, it gives 'ordinary' people access to professional help and advice of the highest quality (or, at least, the best there is) at no direct cost to them. By 'ordinary' people I mean people who are not in any position of significant social or intellectual influence and whose cultural, educational and financial resources are often strictly limited. Unlike the clients of those famous schools of psychotherapy, such as psychoanalysis for example, from which originated so much of our theoretical speculations about human psychology, the clients of NHS clinical psychology very rarely come out of any concern over the complications of their 'internal worlds' etc., indeed they are often uncertain about why they are seeing a psychologist at all. As a rule they are impelled by various forms of pain and confusion which tend to relate very directly to the material circumstances of their lives. The people I am talking about are often unlike those - psychologists, educationalists, etc. - who, precisely, 'talk about' them in that they tend to be relatively poorly equipped to gain a conceptual grasp on their predicament. Many of them are highly intelligent, sensitive, perceptive and gifted people, but are frequently unrecognised as such by both themselves and others. The *most* important thing about them, however, the thing which, in fact, makes 'them' indistinguishable from us all (and the factor, incidentally, which in my view makes the provision of a public health service a moral imperative rather than a luxury), is that if you prick us, we bleed.

'Ordinary' people may have less in the way of resources

than all the various kinds of extraordinary people who tend to grab our attention, but they certainly do not suffer less in the way of pain. In fact, of course, quantitatively speaking the reverse is the case: the fewer your resources, the more painful life is likely to be.

Education is one such resource, and an extremely important one, and what I want to talk about today is the way in which those so often intelligent, perceptive and gifted people I encounter as patients seem to have been failed by their education in ways which cause, increase or compound their pain.

The first thing which struck me when I started to think about this was how seldom 'ordinary people' *spontaneously* refer to school when talking about the important influences on their lives. They may regret that they didn't 'work harder' or 'pay attention', and they may identify such perceived moral failure on their part as the cause of difficulties encountered later in the labour market. But school as an *experience* tends to be curiously blank - perhaps a bit like having spent a period of your life incarcerated in a rather boring jail - a grey period which there is no pleasure or interest in remembering.

This is not so much the case with better resourced, middle-class patients, whose reflections on their experience of school tend to be more vivid and highly coloured. I can think, for example, of several people who had been to grammar schools who were aware particularly of social factors in relation to their schooling, for example of tensions among the pupils themselves. They may have been highly conscious of the advantages conferred by their education and perhaps of the feeling that they were not in fact entitled to such advantages despite having passed the 11+, or that other people felt they were not entitled to them, or that the very fact of their entitlement to them put them at a social distance from their families, and so on.

It is only when it comes to private schooling, in particular of course the public schools, that I can think - and even then not often - of people reflecting on school as a specifically educational experience, as a context of discovery which could be illuminating and exciting. I can remember, for example, a man who attended a well-known public school talking about the enthusiasm with which one of the music teachers introduced a sixth form group to the first recordings of Shostakovich's music, and the electrified atmosphere in which they all listened.

Now I am well aware that this sounds terribly stereotyped, and I have no doubt that if my recollections of my patients' observations have any general validity at all it is to indicate a tendency, not a hard and fast rule. But I would say, in summary, that 'ordinary schooling' tends for most people to lack the intensity of 'extraordinary schooling' in two particular respects: there is less sense of the revelation of a world, and there is less awareness of teachers as mediators of such revelations. It is important to remember that what I am talking about here is what people have to say about their schooling, not what the schooling actually achieves or does - that of course would be a much broader and more complicated question.

For most ordinary people, then, I suspect that school was a time they simply had to get through, that they have little retrospective interest in, and that may or may not have succeeded in the essentially disciplinary aim of shaping them to its goals, most of which seem to relate to fitting them into a suitable niche in the labour market (if, indeed, one could be found).

This is not to say, of course, that school-age children do not learn a great deal, that they do not have a passionate curiosity about their world, that they do not seek to establish themselves in its society with great energy and tenacity. The problem, particularly presumably from an educationalist's point of view, is that the child's curriculum is quite likely to be almost entirely different from the school's, and that his/her energy, tenacity and curiosity are likely to be applied to forms of 'knowledge' which may well not be regarded by official 'education' as legitimate, valuable or healthy. But if their knowledge and experience is only minimally structured by the school curriculum, that is not to say that children invent such structure for themselves; they take it, rather, from the world in which their social lives are embedded and which has been pre-packaged for them by the largely commercial interests which control it. What may look like the *children's* unofficial curriculum may in this way be in fact determined by interests which know better than educationalists how to engage children's attention and commitment. What this begins to suggest, I suppose, is that school for many ordinary people is simply an irrelevance in relation to the world they actually have to live in and the concerns it imposes upon them.

As school curricula become aligned more closely with the business values of the social power system in which education is buried, it may well be that school becomes less of an irrelevance. Certainly most of the educational thinking which is accessible to the lay person (an example would be the recent 'commission'[14] set up by independent television) seems to focus on bringing the experience of school more into line with the requirements of business, and since it is hard even to imagine a school system which was not centrally preoccupied with preparing people for earning a living, that may well have its advantages. But still, when I think about it, failure to equip people adequately for the labour market is by no means the only way in which the people I talk to have been let down by their education. Certainly *they* don't think so: as I have said, they blame only themselves for not having profited from the official curriculum. It is important to add, of course, that people themselves - we ourselves - are not necessarily the best judges of the ways in which we have been deprived or oppressed. How clearly you can see into the reasons for your difficulties depends, among other things, on the availability to you of appropriate tools of analysis. It is precisely such tools which those who have been most educationally deprived lack, and so they least of all are able to say where school failed them.

What I encounter over and over again are men and, more frequently, women who think about their world with great intelligence and perspicacity, but have no idea that that is what they are doing. Far from it. Often the very reason for their consulting a psychologist is that they feel painfully out of step with those around them, and have come to accept what is usually the world's judgement that they are abnormal in some diagnosable way. Their intelligence and perspicacity are often upheld by nothing more than a kind of dogged trust in their own subjectivity, a refusal to give up an attachment to the way things seem to them to be despite the determination of almost everyone they have encountered along the way - at home, at school, at work - to knock it out of them. They have, so to speak, an unrequited love of truth which they seem incapable of abandoning however much pain it causes them.

Such people tend to think about things that those around them, including teachers, regard as not their business or not their place to think about; they reflect upon issues in a way which makes their nearest and dearest uncomfortable. They are, I would say, *concerned* about the social world in a way which others regard as embarrassing or even dangerous. Their concern seems to find no echo, no established structure in which it may be elaborated, no confirmation that it is a concern that could be or has been shared.

These are people who take their experience seriously, but it is too often experience which remains entirely private. And because it is so private, because it fails to find a location in a *consensual* society where it can be shared and developed as a contribution to an understanding of a common world, the experiencer may become afraid that she or he is mad. I remember one woman, for example, who arrived to see me one fine spring morning pale with fear that she was losing her mind because she had been derailed from a joyful appreciation of the beautiful day by passing a cemetery which caused her to reflect on the fleetingness of beauty; this must, she thought, be pathologically morbid. Another woman confessed with anxious hesitation to failing to feel sad at a funeral, but rather registering with interest the expressions of sanctimony on the faces around her. A third tended to concur with her family's view that she must be barmy because she cried when watching Iraqi soldiers being killed on television news. All three of these women - and I can think of countless others like them - were extremely intelligent, refined and sensitive in their feelings, and very poorly educated. What education seems to have failed to do was to *discover* their concern, to requite their love of truth, and to reveal to them a human community, past and present, which would have welcomed them with open minds.

What education is centrally about, surely, is the person's relation to a social and material world. That relation can, however, be mediated through teaching in a variety of ways. Children can, for example, be shaped to a social purpose, or they can be introduced to a world.

The first of these two alternatives seems, unfortunately,

to have become the norm. Not surprisingly in the light of the Business Revolution of the eighties, schooling becomes an extension of management, and prey to all the business phenomena which seem to have infected every other aspect of life: endless reorganisation; abrupt discontinuities dictated by fashion; a preference for make-believe, mediated by promotional campaigns, over reality; the establishment of a system of appraisal which has much more to do with discipline and surveillance than it does with accurate evaluation of achievement. Under the rule of this ideology, children are *managed* according to the requirements of a volatile and uncertain market which trains people to become consumers as much if not more than producers but has, otherwise, little interest in them. Since I work only with adults, I have in my clinical work not yet seen many of the products of this system, so I am not too sure how satisfactorily people are being kitted out for so-called 'postmodernity'. The statistic that in Britain during the eighties suicide among men aged between 20-24 rose by 71%[15] suggests that postmodernity may be leaving something to be desired.

If education were, on the other hand, about *introducing* children to a social and material world, it is by no means obvious how one might set about doing it. Here one encounters all the difficulties about objectivity and subjectivity. At one extreme (and I seem to remember a lot of my own schooling taking this form) you could drill children into acceptance of and participation in a rigidly defined reality and set of social certainties which took little account of how they themselves saw or felt about things but which did have the, maybe doubtful, merit of forcing everybody into a boat they could cooperate in sailing. The ruling intellectual dogmas I grew up with - logical positivism and behaviourism - even if they dealt often brutally with individual dissent, at least assumed that we were all living on the same planet.

The understandable reaction to this form of intellectual tyranny may, however, also go too far, such that people are brought up to believe that they can, so to speak, whistle up a viable world from within themselves, that all that matters is creativity - seen as some kind of inborn trait - and 'personal growth', that satisfactory living is in some unspecified way to do with the unfettered exercise of will ('you can do anything if you really want to'). What one seems to end up with here is a kind of loosely structured 'New Age' philosophy coupled with an often quite fiercely asserted moralism derived from an assessment of the evils of the 'old' patriarchal age of competitiveness and gender stereotyping. The professions of psychotherapy and counselling constitute a crucial pillar of the society corresponding to this approach, since it relies, as Richard Sennett[16] has pointed out, on a model of men and women as self-creating and almost infinitely malleable: through processes of, for example, 'cognitive restructuring', or by 're-programming' yourself 'neuro-linguistically', by circling back through your childhood to complete 'unfinished business', and so on, you can supposedly correct the errors of your history and shape yourself to the demands of the moment. In this context education becomes a question of unleashing the potential of 'inner worlds', and weakening if not proscribing many of the categories of the outer world which owe their origin to the bad old days.

Carried to its logical extreme, which of course it couldn't be, this kind of cultivation of individual interiority would result quite literally in madness. Meaning is a public, not a private construct, and if we didn't live in a *consensual* world - a world whose principal features we all recognised and spoke about in the same way - we would not be able to operate a society at all.

The way out of these difficulties comes with the realisation that objectivity and subjectivity are not mutually exclusive alternatives, but are complementary. The *individual* subject could not be viable, or even intelligible, out of the context of a world whose features and meanings are culturally established independently of him or her, and in a perfectly good sense therefore objectively. At the same time, such objectivity cannot but be the creation of a collectivity of *subjects* - it is in its turn not given independently of the bodies and minds of the men and women who strive to understand it.

If I think about aspects of my own education which I have found most valuable - many of which, I might say, came about in spite rather than because of the official curricula - they seem to have just this quality of reciprocity between the personal and the impersonal, subject and object, and this seems to be the case for many people who speak appreciatively about particular experiences of learning. Something that one was searching for becomes gradually, or perhaps even suddenly, clear through being related to the searching and discovery of others. An intimation of some aspect of the world is given definition and clarity through the realisation that in fact the territory in question has already been mapped by others, or that others at least know better how to survey it. This kind of process is very different from, on the one hand, being forced to learn by rote concepts and categories which bear no relation to one's own concerns, and, on the other hand, being encouraged simply to indulge one's own fumbling attempts at reinventing wheels. The skill of the teacher, presumably, is precisely in mediating the relation between person and world, in acting, that is, as go-between, seeking to satisfy the desire of the person to know the world by introducing to him or her what may in fact be known about it.

It is just this kind of marriage between inside and outside, the acknowledgement that a legitimate desire may find its consummation in an established body of knowledge, which is missing in the experience of the people I mentioned earlier. Take, for example, the woman who was upset by her thoughts of death intruding on her appreciation of a spring morning. 'Knowledge', for her, was almost solely the concern of an oppressive Authority to whose mysteries she had no right to access; her duty, rather, was to learn its rules and obey its ordinances, to treat it with respect but not to encroach upon its interests. Her own sensitivity to and reflectiveness about the world, the kind of yearning concern her social connectedness aroused in her, she regarded as a shameful liability, something that shouldn't be there, that should be knocked out of her, that betokened something very like insanity. When I pointed out to her that the intrusion of thoughts of death into the contemplation of beauty was not her experience alone, but had long been elaborated into works of art of all kinds, etc., she was, after a moment's incredulity, not only relieved that she wasn't going mad, but pleased and excited to find herself in such good company.

Part of the reason that so many of the people I encounter suffer from attacks of annihilating anxiety is that, as subjects, they have long ago been cancelled out by the powers that be, prominent among which is school. They simply are not able to believe that their own embodied experience counts for anything socially worthwhile, and yet, because they are possessed of a mysterious kind of integrity (which after years of thinking about it I still find hard to account for) they are unable to abandon their subjectivity for one of the ideologically more comfortable positions on offer in our society. The woman who cried for the Iraqi soldiers derived absolutely no satisfaction from her concern; moral self-righteousness was completely foreign to her and she would infinitely rather have been able to share the indifference of those who thought she was barmy. What might have been her greatest asset became, from her point of view, her most painful liability. She had just not encountered a world which showed any appreciation of what she had to offer it.

I hope, however, that teaching does not become too much like psychotherapy. For if the kind of ideologies which tend to dominate education frequently lose sight of individual subjectivity, psychotherapeutic ideologies tend to do the opposite, i.e. become so submerged in the subject that they lose sight of the inexorable realities of the external world. By 'external world' I mean that mysterious material and social entity which men and women of *good will* have in *good faith* struggled over the centuries to describe and understand. We shall never, of course, be able to describe and understand it so perfectly that its objectivity will be finally and completely established, but neither is it a figment of our imaginations. Psychotherapies often give the impression that reality is so dependent on the meanings we accord it that we can change these at will to make of it whatever we like. But this simply does not seem to me to be the case: it has been my experience that people are able to reduce their own suffering and distress, as well as contribute to the public good, by *discovering* the truth rather than inventing it, by reaching out to grapple with material and social reality rather than by delving into themselves in order to adjust their perception of it. Our understandings of the world are hard won, and to win them we need access to the powers and resources which make them possible. The fostering of such access, I should have thought, could be a priority for education.

The reasons for our needing to understand the world will of course vary according to our moral aim. As things are, the ruling aim seems to be one of *exploiting* the world to the advantage of a small minority who wish to maintain and develop power over what they have already appropriated. It is not in the interests of this minority, bearing in mind that knowledge equals power, that education should be generally available. A more congenial moral aim - one which might conceivably even capture the interest and enthusiasm of children - might be to use our knowledge of the world to make it a more comfortable place for us all to live in. In which case that knowledge needs to be more widely shared than it is. Which could be another priority for education.

Chapter 5

The Emotional Climate in the Classroom

Isca Salzberger-Wittenberg

Looking at the curricula of Departments of Education and of Teacher Training Courses I am impressed by the wide range of subjects taught. However, to my mind one essential ingredient is missing - the study of the emotional aspects of learning and teaching. Feelings, it would appear, are supposed to be left at the entrance gate by both pupils and teachers, but that is tantamount to claiming that we can afford to attend to the intellect without reference to the emotions. Yet our capacity to function even intellectually is highly dependent on our emotional state. When we are preoccupied our minds are literally occupied with something and we have no space to pay attention, to take in and listen to anything else. When we are frightened we are more likely to make mistakes. When we feel inadequate we tend to give up rather than struggle to carry on with the task. So how can teachers afford to underestimate or even ignore their pupils' emotions? I am not blaming teachers for this but the lack of support teachers get in dealing with pupils and their own emotionality. If feelings are the yeast that makes us rise with enthusiasm and hope or alternatively leaves us flat, uninterested and depressed, it seems to me the teacher's task is to pay attention to his students' moods and to help to create an emotional climate within the classroom which promotes learning.

I want therefore to speak to you about the emotional experience of being a teacher, that is, the powerful emotions which are connected with finding oneself in the role of the teacher. These feelings will stem in part from within the teacher and also are evoked in him in response to the emotions conveyed by the pupils. Newcomers to the profession often find themselves frightened, puzzled, and overwhelmed by the impact students have on them and amazed at the way they themselves are experienced by their students. It may indeed be hard to reconcile the picture one has of oneself as timid and frightened with the way others see us, perhaps as an ogre, terrifying, supercritical, immensely powerful. The course for trained teachers which we hold at the Tavistock Clinic and which I have organised for many years concerns itself with studying the emotional aspects of learning and teaching and what happens at the interface between learner and teacher.

An understanding of these matters can help to promote growth and development in both learner and teacher. In my experience teachers tend to underrate the important place they occupy in their pupils' minds and yet for most of us it is true to say our teachers have left a deep impression; we remember them for bad or good. Moreover, I find that teachers are often dissatisfied with their job because they are so rarely seen as educationalists who deal with the whole person. In so far as the emotional life of the students is considered at all, it is in terms of specific behavioural or learning problems and these are often delegated to specialists to deal with. That, to my mind, leads to an impoverishment of the teacher's function.

I want to consider with you some of the inevitable stresses that are part and parcel of being a teacher. I would suggest that even before the teacher meets a new group of pupils he is likely to have some hopes and fears, whether he is aware of these or not. He may believe that he has something of value to offer in the way of knowledge or skills which he wishes to pass on to others and he may hope that he will have a class which will be curious and eager to learn. But he will also harbour anxieties; these crop up unasked for and have to be dealt with in order to face and manage the task.

At this moment, I have to overcome certain feelings of doubt about my ability to say something that not only contributes to your knowledge and experience but in addition is relevant and meaningful in terms of where you find yourself in thinking about your work. However you may find that what I have to say is unintelligible or you may think it exaggerated or crazy or dismiss it as simply irrelevant. If the latter is the case you will probably convey this by your bored looks, lack of attention and restlessness. Unless a teacher is so overconfident as not to be affected at all by what happens around him, he will constantly be aware of receiving feedback and registering his students' responses. This in turn influences his behaviour, his ease or dis-ease and eventually his performance; and this is as it should be, for to be a good teacher means not only having knowledge but the capacity to get into a relationship with individuals or a group of people and involve them in the process of thinking and learning. I put it to you that here I am already sketching an outline of the emotional experience of being in the role of the teacher. He and others like parents, school governors etc. will have the expectation that the teacher is a step ahead, provides something new and in addition has the capacity to capture the interest of the class and involve the students in the work of learning so that they find themselves challenged to do an important task. Not only are the teacher's knowledge and skill constantly under surveillance but equally his human qualities are likely to be critically assessed and challenged. Bored adults may look out of the window and read the paper. I once heard a lecturer say that he didn't mind if people looked at their watches from time to time but when one actually shook his watch to see whether it was still going that really unnerved him. Children and adolescents will be less subtle in the way they communicate their lack of interest, for instance, by exclaiming, 'You're boring, boring' or 'What utter rubbish' or by sniggering; children express themselves in more concrete ways, perhaps throwing pencils, getting under the table, smearing the desk. I have known young teachers run from the classroom in tears, feeling utterly useless, humiliated and dreading having to face the class again. Others feel guilty when they get irritated with some children and find them unlikeable. Now you might say that if the teacher reacts like this, he is neurotic or too vulnerable. He should be above being affected so powerfully. Possibly a more experienced teacher may react in less extreme ways but I would like to suggest that someone quite unaffected by a group's behaviour has reached a point where he may have developed such strong safeguards against being hurt that he is also lacking in perceptiveness and hence is out of touch with the emotionality of his students. I believe the feelings of being inadequate, no good, the temptation to give up, the fear of losing control, the fear of being judged are part and parcel of the currency of feelings that are passed around quite characteristically between learners and teachers and between members of peer groups of students; and not less so between the different members of staff within an institution.

Now I want to draw for a moment on my personal experience of teaching in order to show how powerful these feelings are and the way that the teacher might use his emotional experiences in the service of understanding the difficulties and painful feelings of his students. My example comes from teaching a class of adults, in fact a group of teachers who came to the evening course which I mentioned before which we call 'The Emotional Factors in Learning and Teaching'. As this is our subject matter one way of learning which I have incorporated is to encourage members of the group to reflect and verbalise on the experience of being students on the course. I have always found the teachers willing to give this a try and to be co-operative. Right at the beginning of the course I have asked them to share with the group what they felt entering an unfamiliar place, and facing an unknown peer group and members of staff. They are always amazed at the amount of fear and worry that emerges, like the fear of being lost and confused, fearing the staff to be hostile, afraid that others in the group might not like them and so on. These discoveries heighten their awareness of what it is like for their students when they have to enter their educational institution. It leads us on to think about the childhood roots of such emotions like, for example, being frightened of the unknown, and to consider how we can help students who are undergoing such transitions as from home to school, from one school to another, from school to college, or to begin a course later in adult life. We consider how anxieties are expressed in different ways according to the age level of the student but remain very similar throughout our lives.

On the first one or two evenings of the course all seems to go very well: the class of teachers are deeply involved in what they are discovering, finding it enlightening, both on a personal level and in terms of their work. But by the second or third evening the atmosphere is quite different. It is as if the floodgates have been opened and pent-up frustration, despair and feelings of helplessness pour forth. I am told about young children who won't sit down and others who constantly seek attention. I hear about violent, delinquent, drug-taking and pregnant adolescents, about unmanageable classes of teenagers, of teachers threatened with knives, of others worried to death about suicidal youngsters. I do agree that these problems are all extremely pressing and I hope indeed that our course will, by and by, provide some understanding of the fundamental conflicts which produce the difficult, worrying and frightening behaviour mentioned, and how one might possibly deal with them. The trouble is that it does not look as if my group of teachers is willing to embark on the path of gradual exploration and able to wait to find out. Instead I am bombarded with questions which come in the form of demands for immediate answers. Here are some of them: 'What you say is all quite interesting but I want to know how to manage my disruptive pupils in my class. When are you going to talk about that?' Or, 'We have children from all sorts of difficult backgrounds. I think the problem is really in their parents. How do I change their attitude?' 'There are children who are just waiting to leave school and get away. I don't think they should be taught academic subjects. What do you think?' Or, 'Classes are far too big and we are expected to get our students through exams. I think the whole educational system is wrong. How do we change that?' Now these are all very relevant questions, and we have had some of them discussed today. But at that moment in the meeting I'm faced with a whole shopping list of requests, and seem to be expected to hand appropriate methods, techniques and answers over the counter. Amongst the bedlam of noise and urgent demands there are some voices of a different kind, like the teacher who says, 'There is one child who gets under my skin and irritates me. I wanted to hit him; in fact, I did hold him in a tight grip, and I wonder why I feel like that.' So here is someone who has a specific rather than a generalised question, and furthermore starts from himself with some perception that the difficulty is not only out there, in others, in the system, but within the bounds of an ordinary personal relationship. This offers a starting point for looking at a problem within manageable limits; in due course this may lead us to understand bigger, more complex issues. Yet the majority of the group are making it clear to me that what is being sought is some <u>thing</u>, some <u>way</u>, that will bring about an immediate and general improvement. While I am certainly aware that teachers find themselves in very stressful, sometimes intolerably difficult situations in their everyday lives, I am struck by the infantile nature of the demand for universally applicable quick solutions.

What was the effect on me as a teacher finding myself faced with such a demanding group? I felt an increasing and compelling pressure to supply something that would meet the group's urgent wishes such as providing clever answers to the questions raised. I felt pushed to produce techniques, lines of action and conduct, promises of cures that would bring about quick and radical change. The emotional tone had become one of excitement, which contained a vague threat that if I failed to come up with the goods, there would be such deep disappointment and anger, that people might rebel and leave the course without giving it a chance. While acutely aware that I had no universal method of dealing with all kinds of disturbing events, I nevertheless felt urged to at least give a brilliant theoretical exposition, one that would explain human behaviour, put it into neat manageable little packages and categories which, though they had no power to change anything, would at least persuade us that we knew exactly how to theorise about it, and therefore make us feel in control and less anxious. I knew I could not live up to the ideal the group appeared to demand, to be the one who provided THE message, THE answer, THE theory, a panacea for all troubles presented and yet I was made to feel that I was inadequate unless I did so. The group was becoming increasingly restless. Some people were talking amongst themselves, others looked bored, some whispered to each other and one man repeatedly called out loudly, 'I don't think this course is worth all the money it costs.' And then one teacher, bless his heart, asked, 'I wonder how you feel? I find that when people are hostile to me it makes me feel absolutely demolished'. I had in fact been examining my thoughts during the foregoing discussion and I am reproducing some of them here because I believe they throw light on the nature and strength of the pressure that can be exerted on teachers.

Such self-observation can help us to understand the powerful dynamics at work, the strain on the teacher when he resists being propelled into precipitate action or supplying ready answers, rather than helping his students to think about the observable facts and what may be learned from them. Briefly, I went up into a spiral of wanting to be and trying to be the ideal the group demanded, followed by a collapse into feeling totally inadequate. This was followed by wishing to escape and hand over the group to someone else. These feelings were all very real, involving alarm, despair and panic. It was hard under the circumstances to hold on to the idea that however great my limitations, I did have <u>something</u> to offer, which might help to throw light on the problems presented. Indeed, once I pulled myself together enough to find a little space to reflect - and this is what teachers always complain of, that there is no space for thinking within such an emotive situation - I realised that what I had learnt in a different context, namely in therapeutic work with individuals and groups, was also highly relevant in this situation. I did have the experience of observing behaviour and thinking about the meaning of it. Furthermore I had learned to consider behaviour in the context of an interaction, to note the emotional impact others have on me and pay attention to it in order to use this as one of the valuable clues in understanding what is happening in the relationship. This realisation enabled me to call a halt to wishing to run away or alternatively fall in with the group's demands. It enabled me to look at it from a different viewpoint; it dawned on me that the teachers were not only telling me about their expectations but were passing on to me the painful feelings they experienced daily when facing a difficult class, having to put up with pupils who are demanding, impatient, aggressive and complaining. I was being made to feel how undermining it is to face criticism, how demoralising it is to be met by boredom and rejection, how frightening it is to be threatened by disorder and chaos. All these hidden forces may be let loose if the teacher does not fit in with the impatient wishes of the students. The teachers were testing my capacity to take the impact of all this and yet go on thinking.

Now these seem to me to be most important aspects of a teacher's task: to maintain hope in the face of despair at not knowing, to convert fear of the unknown into curiosity about the data at our disposal, in order to begin to understand what they might mean. In this instance, I had to resist offering easy solutions as a way of evading the anxiety of not knowing, not to despair but instead try to direct our attention to what might be happening in the relationship between students and teachers and wonder whether I was being made to experience the intolerable feelings of being the one who does not know and fears to be a failure. Members of the teachers' group were then able to speak about how difficult it was for them to be students on this teachers' course. It made them feel stupid and ignorant, particularly as they thought they ought by now to know it all. Finding a different kind of insight made them dismiss their previous experience as irrelevant and this led them to feel incapacitated and helpless. In order to escape such feelings they were grasping for quick solutions, hoping I could dish them out. It became apparent that such infantile, dependent feelings easily come into play when one finds oneself in a learning situation. It is as if the learner turns to the teacher as he might once have done to a parent, expecting him to be all-knowing. Together with such dependency feelings, other childlike attitudes come to the fore. For instance, members of the group were enormously sensitive to being judged, to being liked or not liked by the teacher and the peer group. They tried to estimate whether their contributions were good or not. When I commented on a point someone had made that person felt that I had considered it a worthwhile contribution. When I did not do so it was taken to mean that the contribution was useless and worthless. We could see that the fear of being stupid, being unwanted, being inadequate, being shown up to be a fraud are some of the anxieties often experienced by those in a learning situation; and furthermore that when such anxieties become overwhelming they lead to despair and this may make a student want to give up. Alternatively the intolerable, painful feelings tend to be projected, put into fellow students or another class who are then seen as the stupid ones. Very frequently they are projected into the teacher who will then be made to feel inadequate and despairing. To escape such feelings the teacher in turn may feel driven to give up or else to resort to omnipotence or omniscience. If he pretends to be a know-all, he undermines his students' capacity to struggle to find out. In my case, to offer theories on the basis of the group's experiences and knowledge would not only have been presumptuous and at the same time useless but would have undermined the teachers' ability to think for themselves. You will remember that one person said the course cost too much. It does indeed cost a lot in terms of effort and anxiety if we try to learn on the basis of our own experience and through gradually finding what makes sense. We can only do so if the anxiety of being in a state of not knowing can be borne long enough to enable all the data gathered by the senses to be taken in and explored until a meaningful pattern emerges. The poet John Keats[17] speaks about the capacity to bear 'uncertainties, mysteries, doubts' without 'irritable reaching after fact and reason'; he calls this negative capability. This applies as much to understanding other human beings as to any other subject. We have to start from a state of not knowing, an interest in finding out by listening and being receptive to the communications conveyed by others verbally and non-verbally, and be able to suspend judgement until they begin to make sense.

Often, it is an individual child that gives the teacher a problem. You remember the person who said that one particular child made him so irritable that he wanted to hit him. The child was an eleven year-old boy whom I shall call Duncan. This boy had a way of getting under Mr. G's skin by his defiant behaviour, whistling loudly during lessons and mocking the teacher's Welsh accent. On a recent occasion Mr. G had tried to stop Duncan leaving the classroom and this had turned into an explosive confrontation. Duncan had shouted obscenities at the teacher. Mr. G told us that this had been the last straw. He had just managed to keep his temper and told the boy that he would not be spoken to like this. When Duncan again tried to bolt Mr. G physically held him back and his grip became quite forceful; at this the boy shouted 'You're hurting me, my father will be after you.' Mr. G felt so infuriated that he couldn't restrain himself from digging his fingers into the boy's forearm. He felt badly about it immediately afterwards; he said it wasn't like him to lose control over himself. The next day Duncan's father came and complained to the Headmaster, saying that the teacher had physically attacked his son. Mr. G had not mentioned the incident to anyone because he was afraid of being criticised. He was worried when he was then called to the Head's office. There he was indeed hauled over the coals and told that his behaviour was quite unacceptable; he was warned that if such a thing occurred again he might be facing disciplinary action. During the discussion in our group it became clear that Mr. G felt extremely guilty and yet at the same time quite unfairly and harshly treated. After all, he had not really done anything to the boy. Members of the group were equally divided in their feelings. Most were angry at the father and the Head of the school while some experienced embarrassment and guilt about the fact the teacher had lost his self control. It seemed that we were dealing with a situation which, while appropriately arousing some feelings of concern, had been blown up into a story of crime, recrimination and threatened revenge. This made us wonder what lay behind the boy's escalating, provocative behaviour; he seemed almost to be asking to be punished. As a result of our discussion, the teacher found time to talk at length with Duncan. He said he was sorry that he held him tighter than he meant to but he felt that Duncan was driving him to behave like that. Mr. G then enquired how things were at home. It emerged that Duncan lived alone with his father. When the teacher asked gently about Duncan's mother, the boy became downcast and confided that she'd been killed in a car accident the previous year, almost a year ago. Duncan and a friend had been in the back seat and had been jumping about. Duncan felt he was to blame for the accident. His father had said on more than one occasion: 'It's all your fault. If you two hadn't made such a fuss in the back seat of the car your mother would still be alive today.' We could now understand that the boy's provocative behaviour was a way of drawing attention to himself, asking to be punished in the hope that this would absolve him from feeling guilty about his mother's death. Instead of owning and facing these painful emotions he provoked the teacher to hurt him, claiming that Mr. G was the one who inflicted damage. His own experience had become indigestible partly because his mother's death led inevitably to feelings of guilt but it was made infinitely worse by his father's accusations. It is interesting to note how Duncan's aggressive behaviour escalated as the anniversary of his mother's death approached and how all these feelings of anger and guilt were passed on from the boy to the teacher, then to the father and hence to the headmaster and back again to the teacher.

This I believe is the fate of indigestible emotional pain. We might ask where and when does this passing of the buck stop. In our experience, it stops when there is someone who can bear to hold the pain in his mind and think about it without going to pieces. This provides hope that there is someone capable of facing painful feelings and therefore that they are not all-powerful. The pain is not taken away but counterbalanced by hope and hence divested of its most unbearable nature.

This is the function of a helpful parent but in Duncan's case the father poured salt into the boy's wounds (probably because of his own feelings of sorrow and guilt). What we have to ask ourselves is where can the pressurised teacher, the recipient of so much pain find the strength to contain what comes his way? From whom can he get support to fulfil his task? It is clear that Mr. G did not wish to confide in his colleagues. One might hope that there could be a colleague or a Head who could help to think about such a situation sympathetically. But this is rare. I have met one who goes out of her way to talk to teachers openly about the problems she herself finds in dealing with difficult groups of students and in this way she encourages members of staff, particularly the younger ones, to feel free to discuss their difficulties instead of being ashamed of them. Usually however, teachers are too frightened lest they be marked down by their colleagues, thought to be weak, ineffective, inadequate if they were to admit to problems with an individual student or a class. I know of one trainee teacher who went to talk to the Head of Department about a problem that arose in his classroom and was told to keep quiet about it because, as the Head of Department said, 'We don't want to be known as a department that can't teach'. It seems that an inordinate fear of failure goes right through educational institutions and therefore there is little opportunity for colleagues to put their minds together to share and think about the difficulties they face in order to try to learn from them. This leaves individual teachers lonely, having to defend themselves by appearing clever, having answers rather than being able to develop more insight.

The examples I have brought emphasise three important areas of the emotional experience of being a teacher. These have implications for teachers training:

◊ We need to be aware that the student/teacher relationship inevitably involves some degree of dependency and helplessness and hence evokes some of the more child-like hopes and fears within the learner. An understanding of these emotions is essential in order for the teacher not to feel personally attacked or alternatively too flattered. Otherwise the teacher will be caught up in re-enacting the script of the internal unresolved conflicts which the student brings from his past. If he can learn to think about the <u>meaning</u> of the student's behaviour, he can present the student with an experience of an adult that helps him to bear some frustration and thus lead to his development. (Not excessive frustration but some frustration, which is part of learning.)

◊ Teachers are used to giving out, talking, organising work. It is important that they learn to observe and listen. This involves hearing about a great deal of distress, some of it stemming from the students' experience of separation, deprivation or loss. And I have often found that teachers feel quite unprepared for this because they do not know what to do with such strong painful feelings nor are they themselves sustained and helped to look at such emotions. It would be of enormous help to teachers if, during their training, they had the chance to observe a family, and thus gain experience of how children's and parents' and siblings' emotional state and actions affect one another all the time; how life events affect the individual and his relationships and come to be part of his internal picture of the world which in turn influences the way new relationships are conceived of and reacted to.

◊ The anticipation of criticism usually prevents teachers from seeking support from their colleagues. During the course of a teacher's training there are many opportunities to study peer group relationships. Instead of feelings being suppressed, one might look more openly at them with the intention of learning from them. For example, one might discover how different members of a group compete with each other; how they hide their faults for fear of unsympathetic siblings; how they react when someone is felt to be teacher's pet or on the other hand, thought to be picked upon by the staff. Equally, the relationships to authority can become a focus of interested attention. If this is not done, it may become a hindrance in the work setting. For example, the student teacher who has been in opposition to the staff and subsequently finds himself in an authority role is likely to be very frightened of the hostility he will evoke; alternatively, he may seek to continue to fight authority by subtly encouraging his class to be rebellious to the Head. To allow group dynamics to be looked at and openly discussed requires the staff of such a training institution to be themselves open to critical examination. If they can allow this it will become an important source of learning about the challenges involved in finding oneself in the role of teacher. It will also set a pattern for the student-teacher's future relationships and way of approaching problems, for we tend to identify with the qualities of our teachers whether these be negative or positive ones.

We need teachers who both inspire interest in their subject and give their students courage to go on searching for more knowledge, skill and understanding in whatever field of human endeavour they are engaged in, teachers who encourage learning from experience and who are able to help others to tolerate doubt and uncertainty in the search for truth. This is the emotional climate we hope to establish in the classroom.

Notes:

Chapter 1

1 Dearing, R. (1994) *The National Curriculum and Its Assessment: A Final Report.* London: SCAA.

2 Jenkins, D.E. (1991) *Free to Believe.* London: BBC Books.

3 Smail, D. J. (1984) *Illusion and Reality: The Meaning of Anxiety.* London: Dent.

4 Salzberger-Wittenberg, I. (1983) *The Emotional Experience of Teaching and Learning.* London: Routledge & Kegan Paul.

5 Lewin, K. (1951) *Field Theory and Social Science.* New York: Harper and Row.

6 Smith, R. D. (1992) Theory: an entitlement to understanding. *Cambridge Journal of Education*, Vol. 22, No. 3, pp. 387-398.

7 *Times Educational Supplement*, 3 November, 1995, p.4.

Chapter 2

8 Professor Gerald Grace

9 Hume, David (1965) *A Treatise of Human Nature,* ed. L.A. Selby-Bigge. Oxford: Clarendon Press.

10 Hayek, F. A. (1991) *The Road to Serfdom*. London: Routledge

Chapter 3

11 Buber, M. (1958) *I and Thou*. Edinburgh: Clark.

12 Cardinal Newman (1906) *An Essay in Aid of a Grammar of Assent.* (p.384) London: Longmans.

13 *Macbeth*, III.4, 1.25.

Chapter 4

14 *Learning to Succeed: Report of the Paul Hamlyn Foundation, National Commission on Education.* London: Heinemann, 1993.

15 *The Health of the Nation: A Consultative Document for Health in England.* HMSO: 1991.

16 Sennett, R. (1980) 'Destructive Gemeinschaft'. In R. Bocock et. al. (eds.) *An Introduction to Sociology.* London: Fontana Press.

Chapter 5

17 Gittings, R. (1966) *Selected Letters and Poems of Keats.* London: Heinemann. p.40